The Unplanned Child and the Light Through the Crack of the Door Left Slightly Ajar

The Unplanned Child and the Light Through the Crack of the Door Left Slightly Ajar

by
STEVE GOLDMAN

Edgar & Lenore's Publishing House
22647 Ventura Boulevard, Suite 133
Woodland Hills, CA 91364
www.EdgarAllanPoet.com

All rights reserved. No part of this publication shall be reproduced, distributed, or stored in any retrieval system or transmitted by any form or means (including but not limited to electronic or digital communication, photocopy, or recording) without prior written consent from the publisher.

Library of Congress Cataloging-in-Publication Data

(Edgar & Lenore's Publishing House)
ISBN-13: 978-0998711805 ISBN-10: 0998711802

Library of Congress Control Number:
2017902280

Printed in the United States of America

Cover Art by Barry Simons
Cover Design by Apryl Skies

Edited by Apryl Skies & Danny Baker

This book is dedicated to:
Anyone who can use it
And no less to Sharon Olds, whose lovely and liberating poetry was the catalyst for me to be able to write this, though of course nothing amiss here can be charged to her.
And my profound thanks are due to:

Richard Modiano and Greg Bell respectively
Executive Director and Green Poet's Workshop Leader
At Beyond Baroque, the renowned literary facility in Venice, CA
And all of my dear friends and esteemed colleagues there.
Notably to Rod Bradley and ellen Reich
Who read earlier versions of the manuscript

And to:

Frank Leone, the late Jimmy Gitter, the late Hank Crystal and by extension
All The Boys from Brooklyn

And to:

Harry E. Northup and Holly Prado Northup: Poets, Friends, Colleagues and Mentors, both of them.

And to Karin Spritzler and Claire Acerno,
Grand artists and wonderful women who are in my life.

And to Jeffrey Schatz and bETO Rosado respectively
For the line about surviving one's own murder;
And the line about being born on the carpet and the title of the piece "The Imposter"

And of course to Danny Baker and Apryl Skies,
Of Edgar & Lenore's Publishing House
My most generous and everlovin' publishers of this book.
And to everybody else who offered me substantive encouragement to complete this long, arduous and expiative task.

Coded Arms

The bar sinister means
you are a bastard
in old courts.
You are praised for this,
the underdog is gallant
without an heir apparent,
without gain you become
the common hero, a backwards bar,
~~~~ a stripe in the wrong direction
across your shield, your chest,
your back still uncovered.

Not Bar Mitzvah
a feudal ritual, wonderful,
in communities;
it is an ammendment
the first one where there is
no parent only the self speaking.

MSM

Handwritten poem on parchment © Mardel Martinez

THE UNPLANNED CHILD AND THE LIGHT THROUGH THE CRACK OF THE DOOR LEFT SLIGHTLY AJAR

TABLE OF CONTENTS

INTRODUCTION
EPIPHANY
16

RESEARCH
17

GENESIS
18

DOCTRINE
19

ELABORATION
20-21

ENIGMAS
22

THE TWIN TOWERS
23

CODA
24

HIM
FORMATIVE
25

THE LAW
26-28

STAND IN THE CORNER
29

THE MERRY GO ROUND
30-32

HYDRANT
33-34

HER
FORMATIVE

Milieu
Cast
Cinderella
Commentary
35-38

HER BEAUTY
39

HER JOBS, HER ONLY JOBS
40

BEATING AND "REVERSAL"
41-42

**Dark One Liners 'n Such:
(STAND-UP TRAGEDY FAMILY STYLE)**
43-45

NICKNAMES / HIM
46-47

NICKNAMES / HER
48

ME AND THE LONE RANGER: A CORRESPONDENCE
49-50

FINANCIAL CONSULTATION EXCHANGE: THE VALUES FORUM
51

INTERACTIVE EPISTEMOLOGY: AN ESSAY
52-53

HE CONCEDES MY SUPERIORITY IN TWO REALMS
54

THE ROBOT DRIVER
55-58

THE DRAGON LADY
59-61

NYLONS
62-66

POLIO
67-70

EPITHET
71-72

THE INTERVIEW
73-76

PHONE PROCEDURE
77-78

THE DEATH OF THE DAUGHTER.
79-81

TOYS OF BOYHOOD
82

THE TREASURY OF SCIENCE FICTION, GROFF CONKLIN, EDITOR
83

PIANO LESSONS
84-85

THE PARKA: HER FACE: A RONDO
86-88

TWO NIGHTS, THE ONE TIME
AWOL: THE ABSENCE
THE MOUSTACHE
89-90

CHANGE
91-93

BEQUEST
94

BLUE SPARK
95-96

LANGUAGE
EULOGY
97

PROFESSIONS
98-99

COMMUNICATION
100

CATALOG
101

ATMOSPHERICS
102

**ANECDOTES:
OF WARS AND A TIE**
MY TIE OF MANY COLORS
103-104

WINTER SCENE
105-106

THE OCEAN AVENUE PEACE CLUB
107-108

SEX EDUCATION
109

TWO PRECURSOR DEPRESSIONS
OVALTINE
110-111

RUN
112-114

MY THERAPY FOR CLINICAL DEPRESSION, c. 1959
115

ROY R.
116-117

HANRAHAN
118-121

THE IMPOSTER: A PARABLE OF FENCING
122-123

COPS
124-127

THE VILLAGE:
THE LIGHT THROUGH THE SLIGHTLY CRACKED DOOR
PROLOGUE: THE APARTMENT LIFE
128-129

MARY
130-132

ABE
133-139

BOB
140-141

The Apartment: The Collection
142-149

ROY
150-153

FURTHER TALES
MY BLUE HARLEY
154-160

THE RIDE
161-163

THE NEAR-FIGHT ON THE DOCK
164-165

WORK ACTION
166-169

A TALE OF TWO GUNS
170-171

PICTURE
172

THE WAR
173
WWII ALBUM:
Snapshots, Still Frames: All I Got

INTRO: MYTHOS. PREFACES
174-176

HEADLINES
177-179

How I Became the War: Lore –Personal,
Or **My Complete Environment:**
"The Home Front"
180-186

How I Became the War: Lore,
Or: **A Vet Told Me:**
"Over There"
187-189

(3 Sayings)
190-193

After the War
NAKANO
ANOTHER SOLDIER
JACQUES
194-197

Epilog to the War…Incidental
198-199

WW II Album: Appendix of Alternative Openings.
200-201

GRAND EPILOG:
THEN
202-204

MAIN ENDING
Notes to the poem "WWII Snapshots, Still Frames: All I Got"
205-206

A Laingian* Appendix, Optional
EXERCISES IN LANGUAGE PATHOLOGY
SUBTEXT / HYPERTEXT
207

METALINGUISTICS
208

THE LINGUISTIC ANALYSIS OF INSANITY
208-209

THE DIALECTIC OF INSANE DEDUCTION
The Linguistic Analysis of Insanity: The Processes
A REBUTTAL STRATEGY
210

THE MATTER OF DOCUMENTATION, VERIFICATION
AND SOURCES ETC.-
IN THE FAMILY
211

EPIPHANY
212

End Appendix
213

OVER THE YEARS—STEVEN
214

AUTHOR BIOGRAPHY
215

I who was wronged
By being conceived

…and it was then that I stood up in the theater and shouted: "Don't do it. It's not too late to change your minds, both of you. Nothing good will come of it, only remorse, hatred, scandal and two children whose characters are monstrous." Delmore Schwartz

INTRODUCTION

EPIPHANY

Well, I'll tell you:
What the hell.

When I started to reason it out
That is: when it finally and suddenly came to me in my thirties
After agonizing and obsessing after it all my life –
A single "unified field theory" of my pain, so to speak
I realized that it was because,
Born exactly 8 ½ months to the day
After they were married,
I had interrupted, abruptly, promptly and forever
Their mutual rescue fantasy:
Their respective dreams of escape into liberated glory:
Their idyll.

RESEARCH

Assuming conception before the marriage
Until a sage old aunt   – well into her 90's - -
When some of them want to set the record straight
After a lifetime of obfuscatory lies; -
Said: "Nah, she never would have" -
I knew it was so,
And I reluctantly had to renounce
Even my perversely "prideful" claim
Of being a "semi-bastard":
 -Conceived if not born out of wedlock.

Wedding night conception - or very near it –
Made me legitimate, - just under the wire.
 - A technicality.
The Bastard save only in name.

GENESIS

But it didn't matter:
Even from bridal night passion onward
I was unexpected
Unplanned for
And unwelcome: the interloper.
Born, and then encapsulated in the idea of
The wolf on the fold, the baby marauder,
The inescapable burden, the destroyer;
The Cross-to- Bear
The Angel of Death etc. etc.:
Robbing them of all of their dreams
At the very outset of their mutual escape

**WUXTRY! WUXTRY!
ROMANTIC IDYLL BLOWN
BY CATERWAULING NEONATE
AT 3:00 A.M. FEEDINGS!
REEEEAD ALL ABOUT IT!**
Pace Dr. Spock

They were the proverbial children having children,
Unready and unwilling,
Even unwitting –
But now: obligated.
Hell of a recipe for a family:
This inadvertent blueprint for me.

DOCTRINE

Thus, the central and persistent message of that family to me:
"But for you…" albatross, stone around our necks, unsought for accident
I would have had a life.
Thus, having taken my life forever,
You are the Angel of Death,
The "Malach Ha Movitz!"
So die yourself, little Mr. Angel of Death!

Yes:
Die, Asshole,
Un-be, dis-be:
Run the movie of your life backwards –
Backward through the womb,
To before it – to before you entered it
To before you accidentally came to be.
Accelerate backwards, Asshole
Into nothingness.

ELABORATION

More specifically:
"As unwarranted pariah
At the outset,
By implication
No attribute of you
Is right,
You are equivalent to thoroughly damaged goods, so
Nothing you are or do or think or feel or manifest,
Or hope or hate or love is any good.
So evaporate, Mr. Object,
And free us." -
That's right, Asshole, die.
- This expressed
Of course
Only by implication

Implication of sledgehammer subtlety -
By symbolic talk and action
Whether soft, sarcastic
Or by tirade, by diatribe
Or innuendo in
Endless varieties
Or by sulphurous recrimination
– The Death of a Thousand Cuts,
Screamed or hissed

Not much physical battery though
No less destructive for all of that,
And maybe more
For the shadow of the
Incipient threat:
Of it,

You see? –
Their unconscious was
Prevented from surfacing
By the fact that the cops
And the neighbors
Would take a dim view of murdering children

O: that and the axiom that
Nothing must be visible outside the family,
That, via bourgeois discretion
Had to be avoided at all costs:
Better death than scandal:
The dreaded "*shonda*" for the neighbors

The option?
Seelemord,
The murder of the soul
Behind closed doors

ENIGMAS

Kill you being unplanned
Plan to kill you?
Plan you to kill you?
But all the while the unplanned killing of you:
They didn't have to plan.
They didn't plan.
They didn't have a plan
They didn't plan to have you.

THE TWIN TOWERS

Thus a forked regimen ongoing
Of radiant aggression
Passive from her
Outright from him
Pernicious disempowerment from behind
Overt terror in front:
"*Don't* do it Darling, it's not safe, you're flawed, you'll break apart"
"You *can't* do it, you're a bum, incompetent, stupid
      a liar and poseur."
And if you could you mustn't anyway."
"Mommy Safety"
"Daddy Dominance"
The one seductive erosion
Brutal defeat the other.
The brandished club in front
From behind the anesthetized knife

These the Twin Towers *of* my existence,
The dual stanchions of my life
Jointly and always
Effusing the air
With *vapor of iron:*
Breathing stopped short
Like a puck hitting a door
Thinking without thought
That this was the only
Air in the world
Never knowing at all
That breathing was possible.

I think they call this "emotional abuse"
Allow me to elaborate:

CODA

I was the unplanned child.
Born defined
Not as a criminal
But as crime incarnate.

It was no bargain

HIM

FORMATIVE

*What did I know, what did I know
Of love's austere offices?*
          Robert Hayden

You're a bum if you don't go in the next day.
          Humphrey Bogart

The fifth and last child of immigrant parents.
The only one to achieve a profession,
The only one ever to drive a car.
The only one given an American,
Non-biblical, non-Yiddish name -
That of the then current Irish mayor of NY,
He was therefore the first American
Issuing from a family of greenhorns,
Who, as blindfolded children playing "pin the tail on the donkey"
Pinned their hopes and aspirations on him -

Thus he was relentlessly babied by
The European parents
The two sisters
His biggest brother
And his brother the cop.

Wholly unaware, a man who claimed never to dream,
Though I'd heard his anguished moaning and tossing in his sleep
Which seemed to go on forever.

THE LAW

The first "American"
From the greenhorn family
He became a lawyer
Doubtless to fulfill the family's
Iron expectations
And most probably as well
To have the Greater Law
On his side,
As against his family's law
Of galling disempowerment:
Bitterly resented,
Dutifully obeyed.

From this unknowing compact
And from this marriage
Cloaked in liberation
There issued channels
And targets
For his pervasive occult rage
So threatening and palpable to others –
Angry, resentful, rebellious, combative
Colorful, self-willed to a fault
He wanted to *be* the establishment:
-Escaping the original nest
Of belittlement,
He would be the king
And the kingdom now.

Spoiling to have his way
When he left his mother's house at 32
To marry
Ardently ready at last

For vindication as a man
And openly authoritarian now,
Or since the advent of me –
At latest,
His refuge and his passion was the law:
And I was to become its victim.

Thus I, the interloper
Became a professional defendant
Indicted from birth
And charged forever
With one count of existence:
A capital crime.

Yet I had been convicted beforehand –
The fix was in.
Remember, *"convicted"* means *"convinced"*
- I am *convinced* you are guilty –
- It is my *conviction* that you are guilty –
You are thus *convicted.*

So still the *trial* went on: interminable -
And he was the judge, jury, both counsels, jailer, executioner. –
After his tired and frustrating lawyer's day
 -The subway
His breadwinner's burden
The toll of his adversarial calling
Wherein he could only be
One passionate member
Of the great charade –
Where his combative nature -
His will to prevail
Was naturally thwarted at times.

Now, in recompense, by payback,
He became the entire court.
The entire system.
Of a micro-cult
Of legalist fundamentalism.

The spirit of the law was for him
A calling, a religion.
Let alone the ancient legalist culture of the Jews,
Funneled from Moses' tablets through his Orthodox family
To him.

Now a lawyer, an officer of the court:
Defender, exponent of the system
A holy seneschal,
He would fervidly look
For cases to win
And red lights to stop at.

A defense attorney,
Now I, the eternal criminal
Was his one and only Prosecution.

STAND IN THE CORNER

The usual punishment of choice was
"STAND IN THE CORNER!"
"Stand in the corner, don't fidget, don't move!"
It required that I stand stock-still
My nose immobile just short of
The intersection of the walls:
My own 4" view of the corner at the end of the universe –
The musty, faintly acrid smell
Of the lead-based paint they used then:
The paint-job, - dark green
No more than 3 years old
As required by NY tenancy law,
And I was no more than 3 years old too,
When 20 minutes
Is "20 to life," without possibility of parole.
Every twitch,
Every utterly frustrated
Embattled, terrified grunt
Added time,
And even if I'd done no such
Even if only perceived as such by Him.
The Corner:
There is no time off for good behavior
Or if there is, I don't know it.
"Can I come out now?"
Elicits more time
Summarily
Added to my sentence.

THE MERRY GO ROUND

Long, long ago
Summer weekend/family outing
We go, all 4 –my brother a babe in arms
To Coney Island, place of legend
And onto the great classic Coney Island
Carousel – the definitive merry go round
Of the world
Horses moving up and down
Ornate, filigreed-
Hansel and Gretel horses
Horses of gingerbread wonder
Waltzing vertically to the clangorous
Music of the weird integral "orchestrion"
A music called "brazen witchery" by one writer*
And stationary horses
For the more timid
Or less able "equestrians"
Among us.
Or the littlest children able to "ride" at all, -

Creatures of fairy tale magic
Moored to the platform, unmoving,
And gilded Baroque scroll-worked benches,
For the very sedentary:
Dignified parents
Riding along with their kids.

I am 4 or 5
And I want to ride a moving horse.
I think the War
Still coruscates in Europe and the Pacific.
Of course I am forbidden it by her

"Safety" -
The inculcation of fearfulness,
Erosion of the beginnings of self-belief
That caustic dissolution of trust:
I am primed for agony.
I ride a static horse.

The procedure was that
A hired teenaged kid
Collects the tickets
Initially sold
To each rider
By walking the platform,
In counter rotation
So that you see him coming.
Moving now
Amid the horses.
Toward me.

I have been carefully
And vehemently lectured by him
To tell the kid that my parents
Have the ticket for me,
(No trust for me again of course)
And to point to their bench
Where they sit with the baby
A few rows back.

Again, I am inculcated with simmering dread
Steaming with the dire necessity
Of obeying the law,
And deprived of the means to do so.
When the kid
Comes to collect the ticket

I don't have
I am terrified
And become hysterical
Like a shot
Screaming and bawling.
In abject terror.

And now because of this
I am branded a temperamental kid
The faulty one, overly risible
The "stormy petrel."

HYDRANT

He would take me along
When he made visits to small clients
At their neighborhood shops
Dry cleaners, printers and the like
And park illegally
Right in front
In the fire hydrant's curb space –
A big "no-no" in New York -
I who had been raised
In an atmosphere
Of fundamentalist
Adherence to
And worship of
The Law.

But here,
I would be
Duly and pointedly instructed
That if a policeman came
I was to tell him that
My father was a lawyer
Briefly seeing a client
And would be out shortly -
Thus leaving me
In the fearful weather
Of terrified expectation.

And the cop would come.
O yes, the cop would always come
Wearing in those days
A huge enveloping WWI Greatcoat,
Adorned with 2 vertical rows of brass buttons

And when "Officer Clancy's" voice
Intoned from above
"Hey Sonny yer can't park here, where's yer dad?"
In terror I would dutifully mumble my lines.

And it always worked:
The cop without exception would say OK
Or sometimes "OK: I hope it ain't too long"
And walk away.
New York was like that then.

But "Officer Clancy" was always 9 feet tall
As befits
The Majesty and Might of the Law
So I could never see his face
Above the curbside window of the Buick
From my little huddled position.
Only a window-filling façade
Of the darkest blue wool
Adorned with 2 ascending rows
Of half-dollar sized brass buttons
Like burnished planets or flattened stars
Reaching up toward the cop's invisible head
Which was clearly in Heaven:
The deep voice of God
Remonstrating with me
When I was 8.

HER

FORMATIVE

Milieu

Born at the beginning of the First World War,
Her father the stern American
Already third generation himself
Her mother, an immigrant from Russia at 2
My "nanny"
A loving, benign
And innocent woman.

Cast

For my mother,
Some kind of congenital
Skeletal malformation,
Lost in the fog of family lore
Some kind of surgery,
And a full body cast.
For six months
When she was about 8.
A good little girl,
Compliant and immobile
For six months
A hard plaster thing
In a bed.

How she must have cried.

Cinderella

Curfew is at 12:00 midnight
For her first date at age 18
the event probably long
delayed even for those
early 1930's but they arrive
home a couple of minutes before.
Framed in the doorway is Max:
Her father born with
The blizzard of 1888

Dad:
standing there
in his sleeve garters
his perpetual tie and shirt
arms akimbo
fists on his hips.
turn of the century National Guardsman
Republican
sometime private detective,
boxer
now and forever
the stern Victorian storekeeper,
and hard, unremitting moralist

Dad:
ominously waiting now
his face like something quarried he is
waiting for the midnight clock to strike infraction
waiting for his daughter
to blow her Cinderella deadline
so he can turn her into a pumpkin
which he does anyway in the frightened eyes

of those stunned youths:
catastrophic shame for her
terror for her credulous young man.

Commentary

The message to her:
The world is terrifying, overwhelming.
As you are born
a woman child you are inherently vulnerable –
for you
- the world is a dangerous country,
you may not go there:
fear everything.

Thus was she born, sheltered,
Shackled
"Woman-processed"
As was the dour madness of the time

Inheriting her mother's
Childlike benignity, inherent sweetness
Unable to cope
With the harsh world created by men
And history
Altogether unknowing
Like so many women
Cast by birth into childhood innocence
Cast out of innocence by life into pain.
By pain into fear into craziness
And by craziness into
Loving, wild
And utterly unwitting
Projects of murder by suffocation

A gentle flower born
Who could not understand the weather
And so could only scream.
Skewing foundations
In her children's souls
A little girl
Who played a game of "house"
With her brother, a year or two younger
Around an imaginary woman named
Mrs. Pineapple.
Who could
Mrs. Pineapple
Have been?

HER BEAUTY

She was a beauty, -
Shapely full figured brunette
Not quite opulent the small pewter loving cup trophy
won in the small resort's beauty contest at Lake Kaimesha, ME
on her honeymoon - oxidized, embossed,
gone like everything else the photo, flat, black and white
the pretty, proportioned girl of 23 innocent in
the white one piece bathing suit
standing, posing turned around on the diving board

HER JOBS, HER ONLY JOBS

Only 2 jobs ever,
Her first
A young woman's job
As a typist, early 1930's
The city's Welfare Dept.
the beginnings of socialization,
beginning of the "girls in the office"
cut dead in months
by marriage and babies,

Only a "commercial" diploma from
Girl's Commercial High School,
Trained a typist,
That "woman-processing" again,

Much later
Mid 50's
In my mid-teens
A part time job
In the nursery
In a small hospital nearby
Making "formula" for newborns
And holding them and feeding them and loving them

There, she is a wonderful mother.
As she was for me,
Before I had language

BEATING AND "REVERSAL"

I'm maybe 6
Fighting, screaming
With her.
All day.

Finally
The ultimate pronouncement
(Maximum sentence allowed by law)
As she confesses futility and rage
"Boy are you gonna get it when your father comes home": -
Portrays the father as executioner.

On entering
He is immediately screamed at:
"He did this; he did that,
I feel like killing him!
Do something!"

Tired, crazy
He doesn't need this
But ever the lawyer,
After cursory interrogation,
(I don't know what I answer,)
And finding me guilty,
He commences to
Spank me.
Open hand on the ass
Very hard

Terrified and enraged
I scream
After a few blows

That when I'm big
I'm gonna beat him back worse
For this.
That did it:
Sudden "upgrade"
Now he's raging hysterical
Hitting me wildly as hard as he can

George! George!
She shouts in sudden panic
To stop what she brought on.
Now it's his turn:
His "betrayed angry response" scenario
Raving at her in recrimination
You said you felt like killing him!
You've got to go through with it!

He means they must display consistency at all costs,
The politics of the "unified front"
The ethic of behavior toward an enemy –
Show no weakness and prosecute that enemy
In the ongoing bitter war.

DARK ONE LINERS 'N SUCH:
(FOR STAND-UP TRAGEDY: FAMILY STYLE)

In my family language was brilliantly deployed to prevent communication

My mother and my father and I all died in childbirth.

The faith of my family was "legalist fundamentalism".

My first language was "legal".

I was born "on the carpet" and never got off.

I didn't have a childhood; I had a cross-examination, an impeachment.

My father would vigorously, cheerfully defend to the death my mother's right to destroy him.

Although they couldn't have known it, my parents hated me before I was born.

I came from a broken home, one that was broken internally.

I was not abandoned by my family; I was exiled internally.

My brother had permission to be born; I did not.

My mother gave birth to me when I was 65 years old.

I was born with standing orders to kill myself

I wasn't a good idea.
In fact, I wasn't an idea at all.

I was the unplanned child,
It's no bargain.
(Attention Sharon Olds)

Mad Brooklyn hurt me into poetry too, Mr. Auden

I was born a professional defendant,
The charge: one count of existence:
The sentence, death - The death of the soul.

I wasn't considered a criminal, but crime incarnate.

I have always been stressed, tense, angry, hyper-vigilant, depressive and self-absorbed, because I was conned into another kind of metabolism.

Given the recent medical findings that the fetus *in utero* is affected by the mother's moods during pregnancy, and that my mother was depressed all of her life, I was literally born and bred for depression.

I had two screaming giants to contend with.
My younger brother had three, I was the third.

I was an only child. Unfortunately, my brother disagrees with me.

My parents and my "surviving" brother always liked to think of me as properly murdered. But when I twitch once in a while, it causes them (now him) grave discomfort

When I was born, my parents unwittingly began another culture.

Like everyone, I did not choose to exist.
Had I been there, I doubt I would have approved,
O Mr. Schwartz

I was brought up in a traditional Jewish family, which practiced the killing of the first-born.

Two television co-producers of the day always closed their programs with a stentorian uttering of their names which I parodied into:
Á Bob Goodson / Steve Badson Production.

My parents got away with murder, mine.

I survived my own murder.

They all loved me. They loved me powerless.

If you knew them, you would see a handsome, intelligent, generous, compassionate even courtly couple. And they actually were. They were neither dissemblers nor hypocrites. But you didn't live there and you didn't see their SS uniforms, hanging in the closet,

But I had defected to sanity,
And there is no common language, Ms. Rich.
.

NICKNAMES / HIM

Barrymore: The surname of the great family of actors - i.e. that I was an "actor" – i.e. deliberately misrepresenting myself and things for purposes of wrongful deception, to achieve illegitimate aims. Cf. Willie (The Actor) Sutton, notorious criminal fraud-artist of the time.

Goldbrick: That I was an intentional slacker and or procrastinator, who would delay and avoid legitimate, proper and required tasks. Probably related to "gold bricks" - classic symbol for counterfeit or fraudulent goods, i.e. bricks painted with gold paint, intended to defraud; false goods.

Toiletman: That I would stay in the bathroom vastly excessive amounts of time, thereby selfishly depriving the rest of the family legitimately needed access. (Some truth to this one. There was no other privacy.)

Grapplerman: That I was always touching or grasping objects it was forbidden to touch, willfully in transgression. (Allied with the expression "lobbers" for hands, especially hands as rapaciously misused as above.) Animal appendages. Implies wanton disregard for propriety, safety, legitimacy and the possessions of others.

The Mouth That Never Stops: Self-explanatory: not as regards eating. Excessive talking as regards frequency, usage, esp. talking on forbidden topics, and or willfully disseminating erroneous information. Implying deliberate disruption of legitimate situations and of other's rights thereby, esp. the sheer suffering caused to others by someone who talks excessively.

Big Man: (in sarcastic tone of utterance): That I was pretentious beyond my station uppity, unwarrantedly and offensively so, again for nefarious purposes. Unjustified, *hubris,* properly to be punished, that is verbally excoriated on the spot. Any manifestation of mine he felt threatened by drew this sobriquet, like my not coughing after a shot of whisky, and smoking Camel Cigarettes when I was 17, seen as m*acho* affectation

Stormy Petrel: In fact a marine bird the appearance of which is the harbinger of a storm - i.e. I was baselessly morose, dissatisfied, bleak and angry looking and prone "to explosion." – which itself, should it happen, was another transgression of course. This one was right in part. What else could I be? I still am.

Polio Nicknames: Toe Dancer: (i.e."Girl"). Used when I had polio, in supervising one of my therapeutic exercises. (See below in "Polio"). Hint: Old time Marine Corps Boot Camp, at 11.

FOR MY YOUNGER BROTHER: "Me Too" or *Svayten Tayg Pesach* (literally "the day after Passover, or the Second Day of Passover – Yiddish colloquialism for an inferior copy, a runner up, an imitation, something not necessarily desirable which always accompanies something else) - implying my brother had no originality, i.e. was a robot who only imitated me, with the added fillip that my incessant evil was also responsible for corrupting him. (Young boys generally look up to older brothers, but this did not figure in family matters. ed.)

NICKNAMES / HER

He: (the elliptical "He") – Third person designation of me in my presence, *when we were alone.* Aimed at the some second person whether present or not, but principally a "carom shot" – "a ricochet" for me to hear preceding an accusation, – it being unutterable to utter my name. When alone with her and hearing "He" meaning me, I often thought the "He"- meaning me - was targeted at God, or "the neighbors" or "the jury" – none of whom were physically present of course. A kind of "aside," a soliloquy.

That Older One: Slight variant of "He" as above, but with the added connotation that being the older of two, I should have been possessed of "better" judgment and thus my misdeeds were all the more heinous.

Joke: For years I thought I was Scandinavian, being called "Todd Oldervun." i.e.: "That Older One".

ME AND THE LONE RANGER: A CORRESPONDENCE

In the midst of all this
One time: I'm about 8
And even then struggling
For individuation
I announce:
"The hell with the law!"

A strange, evil and touching thing
Takes place:
He tells me
To state my (anarchist) position
In a letter to my hero
The Lone Ranger
(Think of that)
And see what he, '
The Masked Man
Thinks of it.
Dad will personally deliver the letter.

I do so, asserting my
8 year old's theory
Of the precedence of the person
Over the system,
And, after an act of legalistic censorship –
He makes me say "the heck with the law"
(That is: the *hell* with the law *indeed*)
He takes the letter for "delivery."

By "return mail" the same day,
Dutifully typed by his career long secretary,
A tall Irish dowager who could type 120 wpm

On an old time Underwood Model 5
Mechanical typewriter
He enunciates his statist position –
The Social Contract and all that.
How everyone "cedes" some individual rights to the common polity
For the benefit of all.

Even at 8
I didn't remember
The occasion of my ceding any,
But I would give much
To have that correspondence
Of those 2 little letters
Today.

FINANCIAL CONSULTATION EXCHANGE: THE VALUES FORUM

One classic parallel exchange
Of these sensibilities -

Enraged, veins protruding from his red face,
He pounds the table and shrieks
"You have $10.00 in your pocket
And you think you're rich!
You're "nigger rich!"

And I,
Shouting, pounding the table
Reply
"Yeah? And you've got a hundred grand
In the bank, and you think you're poor!
Who's better off??!!"

INTERACTIVE EPISTEMOLOGY:
AN ESSAY

There were 2 levels to his ongoing campaign of deadly impeachment. It was not just my behavior that was attacked and negated. Just that would have been some kind of family discipline, for better or for worse. It was my underlying feelings; responses and convictions that were also to be obliterated. Examples: Not just "Don't laugh!" But also "Don't find it funny!" Because *he* didn't find it funny, thus it *wasn't* funny; He *didn't*, so I *mustn't*.

I repeat: not just behavior or expression were regulated, that would have been bad enough, but my feelings, interpretations, findings, knowings, ideas; my very perception was regulated, attacked, suppressed, oppressed, and far worse still: CORRECTED. *I don't find it funny, so you are not merely not to laugh; you are not to find it funny, because it isn't funny.*

Thus also with differing preferences. He actually believed that I maintained that I liked chocolate ice cream simply to oppose him. He preferred vanilla, so vanilla simply *was* preferable and my liking for chocolate was *ipso facto* a malign charade. Another example of "my putting on an act" for him to "debunk." I was inauthentic, a liar, prevaricating to secure advantage. I never did know whether I was insane or a villain, my personal M'Naghten Rule* was unclear, Maybe I was both. Anyway I was a faulty machine: a piece of shit with moving parts.

You know, I wish I'd had the wit to tell him then: "Dad, I don't like chocolate ice cream to agree or disagree with your preference. You simply are not "in the loop." I am delighted that my preference for chocolate ice cream pisses you off, but alas, that is a mere fringe benefit. I'm afraid I'd like chocolate ice cream even if it pleased you." That's the last thing narcissism ever wants to hear.

*The traditional legal doctrine (now modified) that the defendant is not culpable if he could not discern right from wrong. The exculpatory power of madness.

HE CONCEDES MY SUPERIORITY IN TWO REALMS

I was a fencing champion in college, and later
Rode my motorcycle jauntily around Brooklyn

He said:
I can't fence or ride a motorcycle,
But if I'd had the chance.
I do both of them better than you do,
Too.

THE ROBOT DRIVER

I learned to drive
In spite of the fact
That he taught me.
His proposal was:
"You do exactly what I say
When I say it!
As you progress
I'll cede
More and more
Discretion to you
With commensurately
And progressively
Fewer commands,
As you demonstrably earn it,
Gradually discontinuing commands
Until you are dependably
Doing it all by yourself
At which point
You will have learned how to drive."

The problem was
That he never,
Never and not even a little
Came through with the latter.
-With ceding any discretion.
Every lesson was the same regimen
Of insane micro-management.
"Now put the key in the ignition,
Now turn it to the right."
Any complaint or protest from me
Or even sigh of dissatisfaction

To the effect that I already long
Knew how to do something
Immediately elicited
The stern, menacing threat
That I'd have to relinquish the wheel
If I continued to complain,
And a few times he actually
Did depose me,
Ordering me into the passenger seat.

(Need I say anything about how this procedure of insanity "trains" one for the suppression, the abnegation of the self, - the pull between excelling, wanting to progress and asserting it, and not wanting to give up the sheer sensuality and status of operating the controls, and causing the car to move, albeit not really driving?)

So one time when I was a freshman in college
At the end of a vacation home -
We were driving to Mt. Vernon
Just north of New York City
To rendezvous with my roommate
Who drove his own car
To return to school in Boston.

I was at the wheel,
The car was moving
I was not driving.

We approach a quiet suburban intersection:
-There's a stop sign up ahead- -
I see it. Dad-
- Quiet! (pause) Now start to apply the brakes-
-Dad I –
-(Sternly) Do you want to give up the wheel? –

- No but –

Stop the car now! –

(I stop at the stop sign. He looks around from the passenger seat, and of course does not see what the driver needs to. "Now go", he says. I don't look around because I've not been told to. So here comes the car through the perpendicular street of the intersection. At the last second he says:) – "We're gonna get hit!" -

The impact is perfectly flush, straight against the passenger's side door, his side.

The blow, at low small-town speed, no big danger of getting hurt in one of the cars, nevertheless slams the Buick exactly 45° to the left of its proper trajectory, exactly at the apex of the far left corner
Where 3 kids are playing
And I'm not hitting the brakes.
--Not because in some wise guy contrarian fashion I'm willfully illustrating the consequences of his craziness
But because at that moment I have no self,
Because there is no I in me
And literally cannot *think* to stop the car.

In the very last second
I come to myself -
I'm 17, a varsity athlete, a fencer,
A champion in fact
And fast, fast, fast.
Reflexes awake at last
I stomp the brakes fast
And hard as I can -
The big, new, recently introduced power brakes
And in a jolt the new Buick thuds to a stop

Quaking and rocking
Not 9" from the nearest kid.
Of the 3, tightly grouped.

At school afterwards I don't sleep for 2 weeks
From rage and the outrage:
Fury at him for being so crazy,
Fury at myself for being so taken in,
My soul so swallowed, so engulfed.

THE DRAGON LADY

So on a whim of a trip
I get to Southern Cal. on my ass in 1970
And decide to stay
And this is a place
You just need
A car
To live real life.
Soon I buy a decrepit
But no less elegant Cadillac
A '55 Coup d'Ville
15 years old, a million miles on the clock
With surfboard racks welded onto the roof
And shark-motifs sketched in white paint
On her front bumper's protuberant "breasts".
Shades of hippie iconography
And WWII fighter planes.
Red, she has been baking in the sun
For two years, immobile
And now her color is flat
Hot, lipstick mandarin-red.
The power windows were
Perpetually open, their motors defunct
But the power seats conveniently worked.
In this rolling satire on wealth
The local Cadillac agency boys
Literally fled at the sight of me
If I came in for parts.
And I got to know
Every local hard-ass
Cop on a first name basis.

One time, in a rich neighborhood
I stopped at a light abreast
Of a brand new bathtub white
Cadillac convertible,
Piloted by the Commensurate Driver
A 55ish guy faultless in blazer
White slacks, gray hair
Impeccably coifed
And those white Italian loafers
With the gleaming brass fittings.

I couldn't resist.
In my jeans and jean jacket biker duds
Long hair, scraggly beard
I leaned out of the window
And said to him
"O, I see you got one too,
 -Hell of a car, ah?"
The guy visibly slumped
At the wheel
As if from a blow
In the solar plexus.

So I called my red darling
"The Dragon Lady"
And true to form
She "disappeared in fire"
When the carburetor belched flame
When primed as needed with gas
When I went to reclaim her
From the impound yard
When I could not get back in
Time to move her from where
She had been parked illegally too long

-This due to the great earthquake of '71.

Through channels
I heard my father raged
When he heard I had a Cadillac
- "A Cadillac he has to have!!?? A Cadillac!!??"
- Translation:
My father believed that his status in life
Only "rated" a Buick
That he did not "deserve" a Cadillac
And how dare Steve, that worthless
Heedless son of a bitch
Presume to arrogate himself a Cadillac
- Making a mockery of the whole thing?!"

A $25.00 Cadillac folks,
A $25.00 Cadillac.

NYLONS

Right after the war
We are at a resort
In the fabled Catskills Mountains
My mother and brother and I.
This was standard in those days:
The small "Jewish" hotel
Mother and kids stashed there
Out of sweltering New York City.
Dads, working heroes all,
Driving up and back alone
To spend the weekends here
Relaxing into pinochle and man talk,
Maybe take a swim.

But this was in mid-week.
There was an adolescent counselor
To shepherd the myriad kids around
- "Give a little relief to mother"

I'm about 8
And I'm playing
With the group
On the margin
Of a graveled parking lot
In the weeds,
Marveling at the sand-hornets
With their chitinous curving tails
The diameter of .45 caliber bullets,
Perfectly ringed with alternating
Black and bright yellow rings
Tapering to an absolute point,
And yet, incredibly –

Utterly harmless.
I am in a trance.

Out of the corner of my eye,
I see Jeffery, also 8
Peeling a switch
From the bordering hedge
With his pocket knife
I of course was not allowed to have one
Peeling it down to its milky green
And flexible interior wood,
And with a kind Zen prescience
I know in that second –
Know, not conjecture: know
That in about 40 seconds
When he finishes'
It will *occur* to him
To cross the lot and
Switch me painfully
Across my bare back
The now whistling switch
To leave a raging welt
Diagonally across
And screaming pain.

I actually see the idea
Flash across his face
Wherewith he starts to walk over
To me, kneeling and shirtless.

A lawyer's son
Knowing even at 8
That I cannot act
Until the attack

Is actually in progress –
That I must catch little shit-bastard Jeffrey
In flagrante delicto.

As the wand
Comes whistling down,
At about the first third
Of its trajectory
To searing pain
And insult,
I uncoil explosively
And deliver to Jeffrey's mouth
The prettiest 8 year old's
Little overhand-right ever issued:
Crack!

The stroke of his whip
Aborted as he staggers back,
Classic kid-bloody nose / cut lip,
And loud bleating
Of shock, pain, surprise
But mostly the outrage
Of betrayal:
I'm not supposed to hit Jeffery,
Jeffery's supposed to hit me.

Through tears and now gasps and sobs
He threatens to tell his mother, and does.
Of course his account is that he never touched me
And that I wantonly smacked him in the mouth.
And you know what?
That was true.

Jeffrey's mother
A little more well off than the rest
And hence the "alpha female"
Of the mothers
And an arrogant, obnoxious
And punitive bitch
Whereby Jeffery imbibed
The same sensibility
Naturally believed her lying brat. -
She went by "Horty" - for Hortense
But the women were unaware of the irony

The War just over then
Freedom resumed,
The insanity stayed at last:
Nylon
Not needed anymore
For air- blossoming parachute canopies,
Flowers in the skies of the War
Lowering their men slowly
To earth for the shooting, explosions
Maiming and death
In France and the Philippines
Nylon, newly available
For the stylish resumption of nylon stockings
So highly coveted; so long missed –
Now the hosiery
Was available again
In the town nearby

They made no passenger cars
In those later years of the War
Just past
And of the mothers

Only Hortense had a car
A new, still scarce
'46 Plymouth
A battleship gray ovoid
Behemoth
With the little silver sailing ship
On the nose of the hood
And this vehicle
Was the only access anyone had
To town –
And the nylon stockings.

Horty took my mother to task
For my provocationless
"Punching my lovely Jeffery"
But my mother
Believed my account.
And defying the pecking order
Vehemently stood up for me
Denouncing the woman's kid
as "that little Nazi in-the-making"
So Horty summarily banished
My mother from the
Nylon stocking expeditions.

My mother would not relent
And this is what it cost her.

My mother:
The female mammal
Defending her young.

POLIO

At eleven
I have polio
Contracted
In the great epidemic of '49.
My brother too.

We had mild cases,
In medical retrospect
Miraculously due
To prior injections
Of Gamma Globulin
For German measles,
A new drug not then even known
To have anti-paralytic properties
In polio:

Four days of high fever, pain
- Transient convulsions for my brother-
Then residual stiffness, muscular weakness
And reparable range of motion loss
In the larger muscles.

Daily physical therapy
From an angelic 23 year old woman
(Thereafter a friend of the family.)
The daily pain of repetitive stretching sessions
Twice per day
The odium of hot baths and hot packs
Twice per day Every day: Every day.

In the apartment for 6 months
Only out of the house 4 times,

Only to visit the orthopedist,
And on one of those excursions
I slam my finger in the car door:
Exponential misery.

But the real damage was elsewhere.

- Of course the sheer ongoing
And maddening fact
Of not being allowed
Out of the house for months –
But when I wasn't performing
My therapy tasks right,
The sweet young woman
Would use verbal tactics
To get me to comply:
I was a smart kid,
Long familiar with manipulation
"You're using psychology on me"
I'd bleat, and then weep.

My step was altered
Due to the shorter range
Of the calf muscles,
Which needed to be stretched
By conscious effort when walking
To elongate the range.

When I wouldn't
My father's approach
Was baiting, goading
Derisive nicknames
In that cloyingly infuriating
Schoolyard mock baby tone:

"Toe dancer" - look'it the toe dancer!"
I was not a Marine.
I was 11 years old.
We had home schooling,
The Board of Ed.
Had a staff for this,
And Miss Tracy
Would come 3 times a week
For my brother and me
Second and fifth grades
At home.

At length
I am allowed
To return to school
By myself.
I must personally report
To the principal,
A huge and scowling dowager
The 8th grade teacher
Of mean reputation
Serving in the interim
Between 2 principals.

I had never been more terrified:
The principal's office's mystique –
The supreme court of punishment –
In any case,
And now, here
I am the interloper, eleven
Who must alone establish
His "credentials"
To this monster of fierceness.

"M-M-Miss Fleckenstein"
I stammer over the counter,
"Yes?"
"I'm Stephen Goldman and I had polio and I was out of school and I'm back and I have to see you…"
"Sylvia" she snaps at the secretary:
"Get the files!"
Who does so,
Scanning the papers she has retrieved from the oaken cabinet file drawer,
On her way over to
The harridan-in-chief
While commenting aghast
"O Miss Fleckenstein, his brother had it too!"
And the principal answers:
"Jesus, what the mother must have gone through!"

And at eleven, I'm thinking:
Jesus, can't I even have a potentially fatal disease
To myself?

EPITHET

A stern man,
My mother's widowed father
Lived with us for the last 7 years of his life.
One day we are riding in the car
I must have been about 12.
In accordance
With the middle class family
Seating protocol of the day
He is riding in the front
Next to my father, the only driver:
Mother and children in back –
(Shades of "Save the women and children."?)

Turning around
He announces
Out of nowhere
That he'd gotten
2 free tickets
To the Dodgers,
The Brooklyn Dodgers that is
For whom he had devoutly rooted
Since before the turn of that century.

To be friendly, congratulatory
Indeed, to be one of the *big boys,*
I exclaim "You lucky *shmuck!*"
.
This is a schoolyard epithet
I'd picked up,
A Jewish vernacular
Epithet from the "penis" family of imprecation.
Implying stupidity and victimhood

But malignity nonetheless,
And *not* what you'd say
To your 3rd generation American
Eisenhower Republican,
3-piece suit, storekeeper
Literally Victorian grandfather.

But I don't know this.
I think *"lucky schmuck"*
The equivalent of *"lucky dog"*
Its schoolyard companion –
A term
Gently pejorative,
Ironic, obliquely friendly.

Explosively
My father and grandfather
Round on me
Shouting excoriations
For this outrage.

Shock, surprise
Embarrassment, quick
And massive pain
Like a hammer blow
To the chest
Also out of nowhere –
I am suddenly
Crying.

My mother looks,
Hesitates for a moment
And says:
"He didn't know. He didn't know."

THE INTERVIEW

One of the older guys from around the block
A year ahead of the rest of us
(Still in high school, seniors)
Is admitted to and attends
A well regarded small university in New England.
Home at Christmas break his freshman year
Sport jacket, foulard tie, pipe and all
He coolly regales us:
Intellectual challenge and passion,
Cars, girls, beer, a drama society, football, sophomoric stunts
And the turning leaves of autumn
In the sharp New England air.
(He is ringingly alive with this,)
He is not the guy I knew
He is in magic; he is transformed.
I instantly yearn to go there
And know I must.

I apply and:
- O miracle –
Am accepted.

But it costs money.
He doesn't want to allow it; *he* can't afford it.
And what's more, -with gouging irony for him,
I'd earned a N.Y. State Scholarship
So I can go to any of the perfectly adequate municipal colleges,
Local and free,
Stay home and pocket $1,400 annually!
The proverbial "small fortune".
He offers me the absolutely unthinkable bribe
Of a new '56 Chevy, if I will relent.

There was nothing in the world
I wanted more than a '56 Chevy then,
Except freedom.

But somehow *she* wanted me to go.
Why?
She, who if anything was tighter with a buck than he?
Did she distantly identify
With my bodily yearning for release –
For the very air of freedom?
My scarce contained hysteria to go my own way,
Out from under the oppressive pall
Governing my every waking and sleeping moment,
Out of some vague or inchoate intuition
Of the same in herself?

Anyhow she prevailed as always,
And he, pettishly broadcasting his resentment
Reluctantly consented.
I remember him sweating bullets calculating the expenses.
Insisting on my applying for a scholarship,
However inappropriate or futile..

I am grateful to her for taking my side,
To him for sending me at all,
To both of them
For allowing me to get away from them.
Yes, this is very sad.

I take the train by myself
At 16, first time traveling alone,
Heady transcendence into freedom:
It is beginning.

My guy picks me up
At the suburban railway station
With his *car*:
- Think how grown-up!
I am in a movie:

And we repair to campus
The dorm – to get me established, based,
 For the weekend of my life.

In the dorm I overhear,
Anticly blurted from a room:
"No Alex, you may not suck my cock!"
This a "grown up" heterosexual joke of the era, -
O how cool!
Nights, I go drinking
With the "boys" at the local college pub
Beers, pizzas, rollicking if pretentious
Adolescent comradery
So big, so grown up, so responsible, so powerful at last!
– Eat, drink and be merry, carouse -
The "glide path"
Toward the ensuing, looming,
All critical Monday.
Monday, awaiting 3:00 PM sharp
Waiting with proper pre-punctual protocol
I'm on the bench outside the interviewer's office.
Already primed and high minded,
Looking bright,
Trying to appear alert, cooperative, even courtly,
Marshalling my "material" -
How I want to pursue knowledge and help people:
My shining, putatively adult self
In my cheap but trusty Ripley's suit -

3-button, dark gray flannel, *de rigueur* for the era
And already wearing a cool ivy league "rep stripe" tie,
Mandated and lent by the demigods in the dorm I was visiting,
Having vetoed my own tie as "too high schoolish."

Swept away by the deliriously free and macho college life,
The intoxicating opportunity, the dizzying threshold of escape
Naturally I have forgotten to call my mother,
To check in: that I am *"safe"*
As I was always required to do,
And here had cavalierly agreed to do before leaving.

The droll, smug, acerbic, Ivy League son-of-a-bitch
Assistant Dean of Admissions
Greets me, as I smartly open the door when summoned, with
"Mr. Goldman, why didn't you call your mother?"

She had called the State cops, the Boston cops and the campus cops, -
Smothering the opening bell of my escape scenario.

PHONE PROCEDURE

So at 21
I meet a girl
Working in a dept. store
Ravishing, blond,
British, exotic.

Callow then,
I was dazzled, taken in.

So summoning my courage
I ask her on the spot for a date
And she consents, saying
"I never dated a man with a beard" -

That should have been the tip off

On that date
Something occult disturbed her
And she walked out, mid-date, stranding my ass
In the street.
Obviously feigning a headache

That should have been the tip off.

She was decorously and strategically disappearing
From a scandal ensuing
From some kind of illicit- affair
With an MP in England

But I'm on the phone with her once
My mother standing hard by –
One partial wall and an empty doorway

3 unobstructed feet away
Doing the dishes
And listening intently,
Listening away,
Shamelessly monitoring,
As she always did –
Never a secret to me.

The one phone was centrally located
In the apartment's, exposed, "public" space
To facilitate just this,
I always thought

The bitch hangs up on me.
(Was that the tip-off?)
I stand for a moment, transfixed
Ashes in my mouth
And my mother says, no sooner had the handset reached the cradle:
"It's no wonder that girl hung up on you,
 - The way you talk"

I don't remember what happened
In the moment after that,
My conscious resumes
With the slam of the apartment's steel door
Like the coming of Armageddon,
Only later to learn
That there was trail
Of broken furniture
In my wake
As I left

THE DEATH OF THE DAUGHTER.

We will raise a family
A boy for you, a girl for me
Oh, can't you see how happy we would be
                George Gershwin

        Madrid falls to the Fascists

I am born on May 8,
That date 6 years later to be V-E Day: - the day of victory in Europe
        Then, Hitler will march in 4 months

But now
The planetary holocaust over,
The couples of the neighborhood
Are creating the "postwar baby boom"

So this is a child born for the dawning era,
A child to presage and embody peace,
Herald prosperity everlasting
A neonate messiah
Born of and for
The happily-ever-after euphoria of the War's end -
The child of its promise
After 50 million killed
And a promise
Of life.
Herself

O yes:
Harbinger of liberation –
For the world
And for my mother:

Her lifelong
Quest for the redemption
Of her gender
Suspended
Surcease of her crawling pain
From her weird uniqueness:
The only "girl"
In the family –
This wound
Cast ever into the future -
To be sure -
When my brother was born
5 years before,
Groggy from anesthesia
When first handed the infant.
She says
"Take it away, I wanted a girl"

Somehow, a daughter
Would be the substance
Of vindication -
Rescue
Feminine projection into the future -
To raise and groom a girl
And vicariously escape
Or at least dilute
Her iron plight thereby
In a world and a family
Of crazy men.'
She would, in a way
Re-manufacture herself

The baby dies in 3 days:
Congenital malformation of the small intestine
Surgery virtually hopeless,
Doctors advise against it
But attempted,
$500.00
My father says he couldn't live with himself
Never having tried…
The baby
So sweetly named Nancy Ellen –
Dies on the table.

My father cries
That once in a lifetime.

Helpful,
My mother wheels around
The other women's newborns
Of that season's crop
From the apartment pueblo
In cumbersome
Ornate,
Black, brougham style baby carriages.

Having been seen around
Term-pregnant,
People stop to admire
"Her baby"

TOYS OF BOYHOOD

Some measures.

I was allowed a pocketknife at 9
The other kids on the block: 8.
But they broke the point off the knife
So I "wouldn't stick myself".

At 10, in its gleaming blue metal cabinet,
They gave me the Gilbert Chemistry Set
I so wanted because I wanted to be a chemist.

But the copper sulfate,
Which her scientist brother had branded "poison" –
Had been removed.

Jesus, what wasn't poison in a kids chemistry set?
Was I going to swallow the strontium nitrate or the powdered magnesium?
Where was the trust?
Ah, safety! -
Too much safety is unsafe.

So I had a castrated knife,
A deracinated chemistry set,
And shame among the other kids

The Treasury of Science Fiction, Groff Conklin, Editor

When I was about 12 or 14, I went and bought The Treasury of SF, Groff Conklin, editor - a huge collection of short stories about 3" thick. Around that age, science-fiction was rampantly popular with me and most of my friends. It was our only "out" to get us as "far away in space and time" as possible from this hell we are living in.

It was $7.50. I had dutifully saved a half a buck out of my weekly allowance of $2.00 per week. (The standard around the block among we nearly 50 of The Boys was $5.00). I thought I was observing the message of thrift, prudence, no; parsimony, so constantly and menacingly dinned into me.

When I brought it home, she hit the roof. "What!? You spent $7.50 on THAT!!?" I'm not sure if I had to take it back as first ordered. I do remember weeping, my little and so dear a project crushed. But I also seem to remember reading it. Perhaps she relented after the tirade had spent its first heat, as was sometimes, even often the case. Well, yes. On reflection I was allowed to keep it.

The couple who owned that neighborhood bookstore where I bought the book, distinguished Viennese Jews who escaped the Holocaust beforehand were friends of the family and my father was their lawyer. Perhaps that was involved in my being allowed to keep this respite from yearning in anguish for transport and succor.

PIANO LESSONS

We had an old black upright piano
And Miss Spargo came to teach me
From "bohemian" Greenwich Village,
Where her husband owned a "communist" bookstore
Through her Coke bottle bottom glasses she would guide me through
Teaching Little Fingers To Play
That most elementary book of the era
And I'd play
In a Wigwam, and *Spring Song*

My mother loved and could play
Beethoven's *Fur Elise,*
She had had sparse lessons as a child.

A tired, irritable, disconsolate kid,
Concentration bored and antagonized me, and
Though surprised I could make a decision at all. I quit.
She said "you'll be sorry when you're old,"
But I did not let her give me this gift,
Her face long with disappointment.

It was one of the few sensible things
She ever said
I *do* regret it,
That these now arthritic fingers
Don't play the piano
Although,
I crudely strum guitar, harmonica
Folksinger, Choruses –
I have not been deserted by the music.

57 years later,
I grieve for the rejection of that teacher.
And for my mother.
Because I spurned
Her gift of those lessons.

I see her face.

THE PARKA: HER FACE: A RONDO

Once, when living home
Again at 20
Disabled out of school
By my terrible depression,
She takes me out to buy
A warm winter coat.

Drawn, bewildered, terrified about
Her mysteriously broken child-son
Her look dry and drawn
Compassion and fear, quandary:
I will always picture her face
So presented in the sun
Her face brittle, pale and bright
In the dry, bleached and biting light
Of Brooklyn's winter universe –
We - Her face.

Her eyes
Glittering caves shining
Holes in the face powder
Buying me the parka, her eyes…
My mother:
Puzzled, scared
So intense, intent
Her look

The parka is a gray and shapeless
Woolen box
With faint blue squares of overlay
I don't like it
Our tastes have never coincided

But have not will
Enough even to know
This out loud
And mumble acceptance
Of it
Just for relief from the burning poison
Of having to make a decision
I cannot make -
No energy inside
The lucent concrete
Which encases me.
Caring that I will be warm in it,
-Elemental mothering –
She says so
"You will be warm in it"
- Wanting somehow to give warmth, feeling futile –
And unrelieved,
Not sure it - the coat - will confer
The warmth she cannot give
The warmth I am immune to,
Inoculated against -
Her son -
Blurred, tiny, distant,
Somehow lost inside himself,
Away from the window
So far away
And there,
In strange agony unspeakable.

Her son in depression,
Terrifying, mystifying depression
Inexplicable depression,
Inarticulable -
No word for it, no concept for it then:

The pale taut shining drum-skin of her face
- Her parched and ghostly look of strain
Pancake make-up. In stop-motion
Her face

TWO NIGHTS, THE ONE TIME AWOL: THE ABSENCE

One time after a particularly violent argument with her
He stayed away for one night
The only time ever

Looking almost unrecognizable to us kids
He said when coming back
"I thought I'd stay away forever,"
 But then I realized: "No, this is where I belong."

THE MOUSTACHE

One night he returned from work
Having shaved his eternal moustache
Just that once –
It was incomprehensible
Visual dissonance
Something wrong in the universe
Out of kilter, weird
Almost as though
We didn't recognize him
And grimacing,
Said as much.
He grew it back
From that night on
Forever.

CHANGE

It comes back to me at a fast food joint
In the frenetic lunch hour.
Apparently the harried young woman clerk
Gives me too much change:
Change for a 20,
When I'm almost certain it was a 10 I gave her.

We were in a market
He's old, frail
Gray, wispy, walking bent on his cane
But not totally gone yet
To Alzheimer's
Sort of distantly rational
And walking through the checkout line
With me behind him
He thinks
The checkout kid
Has given him too much change.
He consults me.
Me!
In his now papery whisper voice:
"I think I got too much back…
Should I keep it, or wha…? "
The few bucks, or the few cents –
The Great Depression
The Second World War
Speaking in his voice.

I hesitate,
I ponder a moment,
What's best for him?

"Nah," I say
"A guy like you
Doesn't need to do that" – I mean
The lawyer, the gentleman
The adequate provider,
The gracious spirit.

He likes the answer
Nods his head "Yeah"
And goes back
To the kid on the register
And says,
With his traditional
Theatrical gallantry:
Only a little effaced
By madness and age
And clearly enjoying his rectitude and stature:
"Here Son, you gave me too much."

I'm back in a fast food joint now
Seven years after he died
"Miss, I think you gave me
Change for a 20, and I think
I only gave you a 10."

There's a procedure for this,
She calls the manager
Who takes the cash drawer
And a reading from the electronic register
Assures me it will take 3 minutes
And she's back in 5
Saying "You were right, Sir."

Thinking "Jesus, I could use the 10"
But not wanting the original kid to lose her job
I hand the manager, also a young woman
The excess 10.

 "Thanks, sir," she says

BEQUEST

Once when I visited him
Nearly 90
Now in end stage Alzheimer's –
Although he never failed
To recognize who I was,
He looked around
And gesturing toward
Everything in the apartment
With a sweeping, down-turned palm
He said, in that wan, whispery
Voice of old age,
That "Godfather's" voice –
"Everything here is yours!"
And that did it.

In that moment
I forgave him,
And he no longer
Rides my back.

BLUE SPARK

He'd drive me
The short distance to school
Before going to work.
It was our custom
To kiss lightly
On the lips
Before parting.
When I'd exited the car

I'm about 10
5th grade or so
And the kiss
Across the open car window –
The static electricity –
Produces
A palpable
Visible
Audible
Snapping
Blue spark
Between our lips.

The next time –
I refuse:
"Dad I'm too old
To kiss" and
I don't want
The other kids
To see it.

In his darkening visage
I see bombers over NY
In rainy overcast weather

I hear old world Biblical menace
Rage and hurt:
"You won't kiss your father?"

In death I kiss his
Forehead 45 years later.

LANGUAGE

For the memories of R.D.Liang and Ludwig Wittgenstein, who explored language and philosophy for blood

EULOGY

As I eulogized at my father's funeral:
We were I said, a family of language fetishists,
Language was to our family
As arms were to the family Krupp,
Gun makers to the Nazis.
At opposite poles of the humane continuum
We were way ahead of the game.
But I wonder.

There was carryover.

PROFESSIONS

My father the angry loquacious trial lawyer,
Language as combat
My brother a professor of exotic
And esoteric languages:
Language as the shield of arcana.

My mother, the housewife only:
The only "girl"
In the family
The innocent little girl, betrayed,
Abused, marginalized,
Taught and teaching fear,
Forever frightened and enraged,
Complaining, ranting, excoriating,
The disempowered
And all-powerful *kvetch* and ball breaker:
Language hysterically punitive.
Language as the lever of manipulation

And I a poet,
Language as pain,
And escape
As anodyne,
As killing family totem:
And false charismatic talisman -
Fleeting redemption / provisional joy,
As art:
Those knightly rides on a great white horse,
Under metallic skies.
Language as music, as sublimity.
As bodily rhythm,
As sensuous metabolism

As song,
For poems,
But also:

Language as suffocating armor:
As insulation.
Language as dope, as addiction,
Immersion
As the aesthetic
And anesthetic
Of the abstract:
The evasion of myself.

Yes, me too.

No one escapes the fetish.

COMMUNICATION

Ah language!
The family
(Where language was brilliantly deployed to prevent communication.)
Sub-textual Combat Linguistics 101.
As Auden said of the just dead Yeats:
"Mad Ireland *hurt* you into poetry"-
So mad Brooklyn me.

CATALOG

In the repertoire:
Language as accusation
As character assassin
As castigator/punisher,
Pain inflictor
As exposer/revealer -

Impeachment
Of the deception
I was continually
Held to be perpetrating -

(Language as weapon,
Only as weapon)
Its only capabilities
Attack and defense:
The "adversarial" nature of language.
As in court where language
Is arrayed as surrogate
For force of arms:
Trial by the combat of mouths,
Excluded from scruple
Seeping from law school
And the judiciary
Into the common life.
Of this lawyer's family
Seen as corrective, educative
At worst a goad
It was in fact
The barbed and lethal flail
Of family injustice

ATMOSPHERICS

From all quarters,
Spoken
More often
Ranted abuse.
If not incessantly then
Hiding behind
The forthcoming moment.

Always
In fear of breathing:
The iron dust
Suffusing the air
Impossible to breathe
Impossible to learn to breathe.

ANECDOTES:
OF WARS AND A TIE

MY TIE OF MANY COLORS

I sometimes almost cry
For a moment -

For the few and little
Expressions of childhood
In the life of
The non-child
I had to be

A little boy four,
I had a little boy's
Clip-on tie
To wear
With my glen-plaid
Short pants Eton suit
When I got "dressed up"

The tie had 2 sets of diagonal stripes
Perhaps 6 or 7 each
The 2 sets of parallel stripes
Running diagonally opposite
And intersecting one another.
Every stripe crossed every one
On the other set.
And *all* the stripes were of different colors.
Thus the little squares of the intersections
Comprised a myriad array of hybrid colors.
No two the same:
So many colors

That I thought it had every possible color:
The great Arch-Rainbow of the world!

I was so proud.
I would tell people:
"See, I have all the colors in the world on my tie!"

WINTER SCENE

Must have been
Very soon
After the war
No blackout

Snow falling silent
On Brooklyn Xmas card night
I'm 5, 6
Walking hand in hand
Beside the blue overcoat
At the corner
A white horse,
Tired
Hitched to a wagon
Lies down in the middle
Of the intersection
Of Church and Ocean Avenues
Resists efforts of the driver,
Crowd slowly, silently gathers
Cop arrives
The cops wore
Sam Browne belts* then
Coaxes horse more
Nothing
Puts gun
In horse's ear
My first drawn gun

Unasked
My father explains
Placement in the ear
Is how to kill the horse

I am very scared
I don't want the policeman to kill the horse
But then on the next coaxing
The horse gets up
And it's over

* Leather belt with additional cross-chest-diagonal-component, as with WWI army uniforms.

THE OCEAN AVENUE PEACE CLUB

At 7
Among the raucous
Vindictive kids
Squeezing out of the most readily available
Holes in their toothpaste tube families,
Aggression,
Little monsters verbally
Cannibalizing one another
In cruel, early macho style
As only kids can.

In the shadow
Of *their* heated family madness –
And mine,
I founded The Ocean Avenue Peace Club
Fearing,
Hoping,
Needing to abate
The epidemic kid cruelty
The intra-group terror
Let alone the organized
Mock, but no less painful
Wars between adjoining blocks
As, now allowed to
Cross the street alone,
Rubber tomahawks in hand
We stretched our cosmos.

Because I was the timid sensitive kid
In a continual merry-go-round of hurt
Unknowingly terrified
Of the rebound consequences

Of my prodigious
But wholly occult anger:
I was chronically too scared
To even know that I raged:
Not knowing, but
Fearing,
Wholly blind,
That my rage if visible
Would crack the world,
I pushed it out of knowledge.

Yes, I was the
The timid, sensitive,
Always-anxious kid
Desperate to reduce
The terror of the world
The Little Diplomat
Who is always the front
For the Crazed Warrior
Of the shadows
Lusting for mayhem:
Torn in two and
Driving toward
The precipice
Of unspeakable depressions
Later on.

Due to lack of subscription
Following initial fascination with the new,
The Peace Club didn't last too long,
One day no other kids
Showed up
At the appointed street corner meeting,
And I was even more alone.

SEX EDUCATION

None.
No mention of it
Was ever made.
Not one word.
Not ever.

When I was 8 years old
In a kid's camp
A 9 year old,
Arthur B.
Confided in me that
Older girls and women
Bled monthly from
Their *"reginas"*.

Naturally
I refused
To believe
Anything so
Terrifying
And fantastic.

TWO PRECURSOR DEPRESSIONS

OVALTINE

About 8.

Between the 6 storey
Brick or stone apartment massifs
Were basement level corridors -
Separating them,
Narrow, dank,
Concrete floored
Exposed to the sky.

They functioned as
"Kid-secret" shortcuts
Between parallel streets
When playing
We went from "in front"
To "out back"
On our urgent
Secret missions.
Running
In small packs.

A time came
When I felt
I couldn't keep up
With the rest.
Not out of breath,
Not physical:
I just couldn't keep up.

The radio,
Sponsoring "Capt. Midnight":
"KIDS! No pep? Can't keep up with the gang? Ask your mom for
OVALTINE: packed with vitamins and minerals for energy!"
Diagnosing an Ovaltine deficiency,
I asked my mom for
Ovaltine -a kind of vaguely chocolate milk additive.

The Ovaltine tasted awful
It tasted like straw
And it didn't work.

RUN

17 years old
The summer between high school and college.
Going away, at last!
So long yearned for, so cherished.
But I can't go out of the house.
Lassitude, chronically frightened
Of nothing known
Fearing I harbored ineffable
Fatal illness.
-That I would break
And die
From the slightest exertion.

Rounds of doctors,
And tests.
Nothing.
No word for,
No idea of
Depression then.

The last resort:
I am taken to a doctor
"Up the block", - a few buildings away
MDs had offices in their apartments then
- An eminent man
The Chief of Service of
The Dept. of Internal Medicine
In the Brooklyn Jewish Hospital
Where I had been born 17 years before.
A crusty Jewish bachelor
Married to medicine:
A guy out of a movie.

He examines me
With great and thoughtful thoroughness
And then does the unprecedented –
The inconceivable!
He gruffly but properly
Orders my mother from the room.
Banishes Her!
Unthinkable.

We talk privately,
And he tells me that nothing's the matter with me physically
And in simple, kid terms - but smart kid terms -
How sometimes when we worry too much
Or are about to make a big change in our life
We can get very downhearted,
And stay that way.
And think we are sick.

In looking back
I quail to think
Of that man's human wisdom, -
Of what he knew.

That did it!
Then and there!
It broke the depression:
My death sentence had been commuted!

I went right out
And ran around the big block
As fast as I could,
Twice!
AND I WAS ALL RIGHT!
I who was going to die

If I coughed too hard.
And I as all right until 2 years later
In college at 19
When it all started in earnest
And there was no recourse

MY THERAPY FOR CLINICAL DEPRESSION, c. 1959

"Get outta' bed
Ya bum,
And getta job!
Or go back to school!

Somethin'!"

ROY R.

In the 5th grade, a new kid was transferred in. He was newly pubescent and none of the rest of us was. He towered a head above me. He dressed in that zoot-suit derived gear *de rigueur* for boys in the early 50s needing to look cool and tough, if their mothers would let them: pastel pegged pants with saddle-stitching down the sides, a "gaucho" shirt with the collar up of course, and the era's obligatory "duck's ass" hairstyle. He was sexually conscious. Boy, was he ever cool, changing voice and all. He was a bully and naturally he singled me out, as bullies always have.

I was still a little pre-adolescent dough-boy, who still wore kid's clunky "pepper and salt" corduroy pants, which went "woovwoovwoov" when you walked as the ridged thighs abraded one another.

He continually picked on me in class, and in those days, some of the more craven teachers, unable to cope with the class bully, would "buy him off" my making him a "class monitor" – read "kid-cop" – invested with her authority over the rest of us. I had no succor.

And he would beat me up every Friday at 3:00 P.M., as the teachers were fleeing for their cars or the subway. This ritual became the weekly schoolyard social event.

I was always terrified and always cringed away, thinking that any certainly futile attempt at retaliation would egg him to even greater violence. 3 or 4 weeks went by in this fashion, as the attendant circle of kids laughed and jeered at me, and cheered him on.

But the final time, I lost my temper. I swung 2 looping, ineffectual, virtually girlish overhand rights at his face, and missed by a foot each time. But I will never forget his face. He stopped punching. His jaw dropped. Surprise, incredulity above all, hurt at *betrayal*! I wasn't sticking to the script! Roy was supposed to punch *me*; I wasn't supposed to punch *him*! He slowly turned and walked away, crestfallen in real disappointment. There were no more Friday beatings.

I swore to myself that if I ever encountered him when I was grown up, I would tear his arms and legs off. That is actually how I phrased it to myself.

Flash forward about 10 years. I am going to a movie in a local theater at night by myself, a young man alone, disconsolate and 21. I might have seen Ava Gardner in The Barefoot Contessa. Between features, I am ascending the small flight of stairs from the balcony to the mezzanine level bathroom above when, in the middle of the stairway: there he is! Coming down! He hadn't grown an inch, still 5'2", and I had long ago attained my adult stature, about 5'10". Recognition is instant, simultaneous and electric! I see his face suddenly and palpably whiten. We are both stopped in our tracks, *en face,* mid-stairway.

Oh, I considered it all right. But I realized that the theater management, let alone the cops, would take a dim view of my spontaneously beating the shit out of someone half my size, in a public place at that, over a schoolyard "beef" a decade old.

So I smiled my best, flattened Richard Widmark soulless killer's smile at him, held stark for a breathless moment: a deadly smile of complete sadistic satisfaction. And I walked on by.

I later found out that he was one of those kids who had been administered "hormone shots" – a thing in vogue then, available to mothers who thought their kid's puberty was late. Probably testosterone, it surely did induce puberty, but was later implicated in conferring shorter stature on the individual than he otherwise would have had.

HANRAHAN

In early high school
Due to some kid "affair of honor"
The specifications of which I will never remember –
The classic "I'll see you after school!" fight was arranged
Between me and Hanrahan -
A short, spindly, acned little Irish kid.
Whom I towered over and massively out-bulked.
Whom I could have "beat the shit out of"
And even knew it.

We were to meet of course
At the Flatbush Avenue
Main portal to the school
That gray stone "Flatbush Arch" –
The school's classic dueling ground
For such matters.

Size or no
Of course I was terrified anyway
But given the rigid, pervasive
Kid – code -
(And not all women understand this)
I could not fail to appear
And be branded a "chicken"
Forever.

At the assigned hour
I showed up,
Ever the Lone Ranger,
Alone
Quashing down the fear deep in my gut:
"Macho" appearance at all costs.

Of course there was Hanrahan
Who could no more back out
Than I,
Visibly shaking
With ill-concealed
Terror of his own,
But accompanied
By 4 or 5 of his
Clannishly gathered
Bellicose-faced or smirking
Proto- thuggish Irish kid friends
As "seconds"
Some of them
My size,
And more.

The code required
That they not interfere
No matter what the progress
Of the fight,
Unless it was deemed
That I had
Some unfair advantage
And little Hanrahan
Was entitled to help -
As for example,
If I were winning
He was losing:
Even fairly.

Seeing this poor kid quake
It came to me
To state that
I did not want to fight

That I saw it
As unwarranted
And admitted to some
Of their charges
Asserting that
It was all or mostly
All a misunderstanding.
All
Without
Showing fear
And keeping
My manner composed.

If we fought
I was fucked, win or lose.
Win, I'm a bully
For taking advantage of little Hanrahan
And my crime would be avenged:
His pals would promptly
Kick my ass *en masse*.

Lose to such a little guy
And I'm a wimp.
Even if not a chicken altogether.
And I was not prepared to feign losing.
That would have been just too much.

I prevailed.
They conferred,
Hanrahan and his allies –
And the fight was called off,
Everybody's honor satisfied.
Even if minimally.

Stifle it though they tried,
I could see
The relief
On Hanrahan's
Face
And even on those
Of his small army.

THE IMPOSTER: A PARABLE OF FENCING
With thanks to beto Rosado

In college, I was on the fencing team. In a stylized white suit, with a make-believe sword in hand and a steel mesh for a face, I would face another anonymous youth on a strip two meters wide that stretched away into infinity, as in a dream. I would duel with Abstraction. I was pretty good though; I won most of my bouts. I was nineteen and too scared to lose.

But I got no satisfaction. When I'd lose, about a third of the time, I'd feel bad: *O why didn't I evade that attack instead of trying to parry it? O how could I let this guy beat me, I am so much better than he is!*

When I'd win, about the other two thirds of the time, - a very good record incidentally – I'd feel - Nothing. Anesthesia. Only: *O, so what? You won a fencing bout. What's the big deal?* The whole thing was vaguely annoying.

Once the following actually happened to me. I was in a bout with a kid, tied 4-4 when the time limit of five minutes expired. Fencing is very strenuous. In *epee* fencing, which allows simultaneous touches to count, simultaneous touches in this situation result in defeats for both parties. This is the only sport where this double-defeat protocol obtains, because its inventors wanted to keep it as close as possible to actual dueling. In this "sudden death" situation, a conclusive attack must be conservatively chosen and virtually certain. Now the bout had run uninterrupted to an additional fifteen minutes. Unheard of! The gym was stock still, and the only sound audible was my heaving breathing, like that of a racehorse run a mile and three quarters.

I noticed that the other guy, a little less experienced, was arm-weary and carrying his weapon a little low. In great pain and now more to get out of this than anything else, to stop this ordeal one way or the other, I conceived a do-or-die attack I'd never been taught, exploiting his slight vulnerability. I feinted low to draw the attention of his already too low blade, and with a large semi-circular rising deception threatened his now unguarded upper chest, and lunged instantly. Long classic lunge, perfectly executed attack, and nailed him.

Explosive deafening roar. Sustained. My teammates tensing forward anyway pour off the bench and the next thing I know I am up on the shoulders of these big football players who had come out for fencing in the off-season. Think of that: *Jack Armstrong of Yale, carried from the field of honor on the shoulders of his mates!* This actually happened to me.

And what am I feeling there, up in the air like a Jewish bride? Nothing. *Jesus, what's this all about? What planet am I on?* All I wanted to do was fight my way down to salute the other guy and shake hands, which you are supposed to do.

The Impostor had won the fencing bout. Not me.

COPS

Long time later In my 30's
New home, far away, the
Other coast of the moon no
School, no collared job
No rush hour

A construction worker
Now (and will be 15 years) a
Laborer free to write poems

Out drinking with
"The boys" from the crew on
A typical night wending
Home very drunk
Through the alley by the sea.

On the hunt a police car,
Smelling blood abruptly
Pokes its snout into the alley
I am traversing
And jounces to a stop
I stop too, a little startled,
And perceive it to be a question
Of who will go first? –
Me in the direction I'm going
Or him, on the right turn
He must make into
The one-way "T-bone" intersection

A New Yorker, a wise-ass
Versed in jovial silliness
(and very drunk, as noted)

And being, I thought –
Courteous, I cede him the
Prerogative
Bow fractionally at the waist
Passing my upturned palm
Across my waist
In the direction he will go
In the classic courtly manner, -
Sure, now a little burlesque
As in "after you Alphonse."

That is all it takes
The driver
(Very cop-harsh):
Shouts What's that in your hand?
A cigar.
Drop it!
I do.
They pile out of the car
One grabs me in bear hug embrace
Just as 2 more cars
Lovely cop car choreography
Come synchronously screeching
Around the two bracketing corners,

Two more cops each pile of out each
Six altogether
One comes and joins in the now
Double bear hug
And the first of the original two
Begins punching me
Hard.
Perfectly vertical uppercuts
Under the balls,

Surgically perfect,
Screaming pain: no lasting damage.
The Gestapo in blue
Is letting me know who they are:

The three remaining cops
Have fanned out 5 feet
In a surrounding circle
Hands on pistol butts.
I realize instantly that
These cocksuckers will shoot me if I resist,
Let alone retaliate.

Involuntarily
I yelp loudly
With each blow

Then, only then
Do they requisition and inspect
My "ID"
Muttering disappointment
That I'm not the guy they want
The original two
Get back in their car
And start to drive away

I "mouth off"
"Hey you!"
The passenger cop, gruffly, sarcastically:
"Yeah?"
"You owe me a cigar."

You have to salvage something.

For 2 weeks
I am looking for these guys
With mayhem in my heart.
But eventually I realize
That with their impeccable razor creased uniforms
Identical British air force mustaches
As if out of an aerosol can
And steely looks
In their eyes
Lacquered over
Dancing sadism–
I can't even tell them apart
Let alone identify them,
- And that stalking uniformed
Police officers
In broad daylight
With the object
Of beating the living shit
Out of them
Would not exactly
Be a "growth industry"
For me.

But I had learned something about rape,
And such learning is a wound.

THE VILLAGE:

THE LIGHT THROUGH THE CRACK OF THE DOOR LEFT SLIGHTLY AJAR

It takes a whole village to raise a child.
African Tribal Proverb

PROLOGUE: THE APARTMENT LIFE

Had it not been
For 4 ancillary individuals,
The dowager Irish lady
Living next door;
My paternal uncle,
The sometime PDNY
Chief of Detectives
Of Brooklyn NY;
My cousin
His son:
A captain, United States Navy
And submarine commander;
And a male first cousin
Of my mother's
By marriage;
I could not have come to be.

The one standing pane of light
Squeezing through the slightly open
The slightly "cracked" door
Because of them -
Not illuminating anything particularly
But just suggesting that
Things and consciousness

Could be irradiated –
And seen to be done differently
In the adult world:
Because a kid
Growing up
Thinks his apartment
And its ways
Are the universe.

They were the "whole village"
It took to raise me –
Out of the ashes
Of myself.

Mary, Abe, Roy, Bob.

MARY

Proper, prim, restrained
She was petite
Single, strong willed
Red headed with the best and subtlest
Touch up job then available,
Irish as all hell.
Self made "lace curtain" Brooklyn Irish
Up from nothing -
The administrator
Of a small Catholic hospital nearby:
The lonely boss.
In her small-neat-as-a-pin
Apartment next door
Beautifully appointed
-   The Della Robia ceramic
Of the Virgin -
Blessed by the Pope.
Think of it:
The Virgin Mary:
She was
Like so many Irish Catholic
Women of her day
Who didn't marry:
A secular nun.

A career spinster,
She was in lifelong love with
The principal
Of a prosperous chain of Irish Catholic funeral homes,
Brooklyn wide,
And he with her.
So the story went.

But he'd been divorced
So they never could marry
-The Church was draconian severe
About such things
In New York then.

I think I was the child she never
Was to have,
Or raise.
-And yet she did.
It was as simple
And redemptory and powerful
As this:

When I'd been abused
Made crazy,
Maddened to excruciation
I'd storm out of the apartment
At least once with an
Unperceived gauntlet
Of broken furniture
Following in my blind
And roaring wake.
With murder in my heart
And almost in my hands.
I'd slam the heavy steel
Apartment "safety" door
With all my 17-year-old athlete's force
The resultant crash titanic:
The Viconian thunderclap
At the end of the world.

At this building shaking blast
And as her own apartment shook

She'd open her adjoining steel door
Just a crack so *They* wouldn't see
And whisper: conspiratorial,
So as not to be heard
By *Them*:
"Stephen, come in and
Have a drink with yer Aunt Mary."
I would,
The one scotch
And only the one, of course
And we'd talk
As my respiration
Descended to human levels
About how imperfect
They were, we *all* were,
But all the while
Fully acknowledging
My pain
Its extent,
And above all
Its legitimacy,
And mine:
With the attempt at life instruction
Concomitant recognition
Of me as human,
As worthy:
Pure true love:
A friend, a mother:

The crack in the doorway –
Light.

ABE

My uncle, the cop -
The Jewish cop
The Chief of Detectives
Brooklyn, NY –
This through the late 1940's
And my father's older brother:
He was the archetype
Of the stereotype
Of the NY detective Of the era.

Short of stature
But heavy set
Baggy rumpled double-breasted suit
Woolen overcoat almost to his ankles
Al Capone style "bomb thrower" hat
Omnipresent cigar a part of his facial anatomy
Deep, resonant gravelly, sarcastic loving voice.
Tough, gruff, tender, sentimental,
Colloquial, funny,
Ironic and ironically witty
Poetic,
Creatively sarcastic at need:
Cop style
And loving underneath it all.
You know the drill:
A real life
Humphrey Bogart.

One time
A fugitive killer,
A black guy
Named Major Green
Was holed up in a room

In Coney Island
Or some place
Armed and
Swearing never to be taken alive.
My uncle said:
"Major, I'm comin' in after yuh"!
And Major Green said:
"Well, Abe, since it's you,
 I'll surrender."
And he did: the arrest was made.
In those days
Cops and bad guys
Were on a first name basis
Even crime was more civilized then
Allowing this gallant exchange

But Major Green went to
"The chair" for his troubles,
And my uncle,
Who did not believe
That this should happen
Wept like a baby
Through the night
Of the execution.

My uncle had the soul of a poet.
He'd recite long swatches of
Robert Service and Rudyard Kipling
Those perennial gritty, musical
Male favorites,
And once himself composed
A long, risqué, hilarious and perfect
Parody of a Service poem

Which I would give empires for
Now
Could I but remember
One line.

His apartment
A block away from us
Shared with his wife
My Aunt Lilly
Was distinctive too.
None of the overstuffed
Furniture nor rich
Broadloom carpet
So typical
Of petty bourgeois
Jewish Brooklyn then,
Instead, spare
But serviceable furniture,
Bridge tables
Straight backed chairs and the like
Well-kept bare wooden
Parquet floors.

Eccentrics, devoted
Not to "proper" furnishings"
But sports:
They were friends with
The Brooklyn Dodgers, the N.Y. Rangers, the N.Y. Knicks, the
then Brooklyn Football Dodgers and the N.Y. Football Giants,
Joe Louis, etc.
(The cops always had complimentary tickets in those days)
But they, especially my aunt,
Were privately castigated for this
By other women in the family/neighborhood,

But none dared
Openly admonish
The virtual "Chief of Police"
Of Brooklyn, N.Y.
In that colorful,
Formative, urban
Era.

I was their
Only visitor ever
From the family -
Due to their subtle Ostracism.
I'd run there too,
In craziness.

"Ahh, ya bum":
He'd croak,
(His loving voice
The sound of
A tin garbage can lid
Dragged over gravel)
He'd greet me thus
With his favorite
Nickname/epithet for me,
Invite me in
And offer me a drink –
A towering adult honor to me
At 16.

And the first such time
As I raised my glass to drink
He said "Ahhya bum:
Don't ya drink to a guy's health

When he "buys" ya a drink?!"
In this one stroke
He was relating me
At once and forever.
To the world
Of human social custom,
Of human doing and involvement,
And with this one gesture,
My true Bar Mitzvah,
I began
To find a place in the world:
The only price
That one moment
Of chagrin
At my social virginity.

But it had now
Been intimated to me
However vaguely,
That I just might barely be
An adult, sentient, competent
A varsity player, a voter,
A citizen, a social entity
In a word, I existed,
I counted.

I have never missed
Toasting the "buyer" since.

In his day
(The 20's)
He'd been the Light Heavyweight Champion
Of the New York Police Dept.
A rank equivalent to "pro"

And this amongst a population
Of fistically savvy Irishmen.
His involvement with "the game"
Was such that he worked
Joe Louis' corner
On the "sly".
Because serving cops
Can't publicly back
One guy or another –
Conflict of interest / appearance of impropriety - -
This indicative of his humanized rule-bending,
So unlike the manic legalism
Of lesser cops and bureaucrats
-A precious and pervasive lesson in itself.

And once, on a family outing
In the suburban driveway of a relative's
House on a warm spring day
He, now long retired
-When I
Just back from
Graduate school in Canada
With a solid year
Of karate practice
And in the best shape
Of my life before or since, -
Made a mock challenge-
"Put 'em up, Inspector" –
Invoking that open-handed
Barely contacting soft sparring kids always do
Implying "see what I could'a done if this was real"
-Thinking I could show off
How fast and adept I was

- And I was fast and adept –
And impress him thereby.
After all
He was 72
And I 25.
I put up my hands.

Next thing you know
There's the side of his fist
In my face
Which I simply did not
See coming or originating:
A roundhouse sucker punch
With which he didn't actually hit me
Of course, but stopped an inch short.

Precious lesson:
Don't underestimate anybody:
Assumptions are always dangerous.

He could have knocked my head off.

Light, light:
The crack in the doorway

BOB

Bob

The gallant husband of my mother's close first cousin
Full white wavy hair
His voice, very basso deep; very, very slow, very considered, deliberate
Impeccable waxed white handlebar mustaches,
As late as the century's 90's,
And his:
Mark Twain, imperially slim, as they say.
Elegant, courtly manners, considerate, compassionate
A cavalier of sorts, a southern gentleman of the north
A man of another era and sensibility:
Aestheticism his defining devotion
He was, above all,
The Man of Consummate Taste

Amulet

A collector, a connoisseur of beauty:
This was the passion of his life.
He wore, on a thong around his neck
An amulet of carved Chinese jade
"Tomb jade", he always averred,
The finest, rarest kind.
It was simply that he loved it, and what it stood for:
Beauty, artisanship, culture,
Beauty as cultural bi-product,
Culture as bi-product of beauty,
Culture and beauty as the anodynes
Of human pain:
Art: inducer of the spiritual.

No social dress convention of his era,
So rigidly "suit and tie" stylized
As such,
He himself
Was a small billboard advertisement for beauty,
For grace -
A fellow artist's sensibility –
About form rendering
Beauty rendering
Aesthesis –
The leap of the spirit
The joy of the heart.

The Apartment: The Collection

Chairs

His apartment of 65 years
Was a dark 'brown study'
Museum of objects:
Massive and lowering
Carven Chinese chairs,
Dark of wood, richly figured, somber
From whatever dynasty,
And square
Which made you sit expansively upright
On seats of cool stone
Under your ass -
- To encourage thinking.
 He said.

Painting

A Turner seascape,
Small boats in a harbor
At dusk.
Magnificent,
The sails riotously colored
The sky the color of gore
- The provenance of which
The family always contested
Needing to "unseat" him
To render their own
Conventional lives justifiable.

Box

And best of all for me
Whenever we visited
(I'd ask that he get it out) –
A box, a small box
About the size of a box
Of wooden matches
Faberge
Covered in gorgeous
Deep toned
Parti-colored enamels
Intricately worked
- Gold wired cloisonné,
With a nickel sized hatch
Center top
-Still cloisonné
Which, when the underside
Switch was pushed
Would flip up
And up would pop
A tiny hummingbird! -
Real feathers,
Bright colors right,
The ½" bird
Excruciatingly accurate
Would twirl
And dance around
To seven different
Perfect mellifluous birdcalls
All driven
By the gleaming brass
Swiss wind-up music-box movement
Underneath.

The Visual and Me

Though never much concerned myself
With plastic or visual art objects
This is still
The single most
Thrilling such object
I have seen,
And what is more:
He taught me how to see.

Fountain Pen

At my Bar Mitzvah,
At the party after the party
Now in our apartment,
He presented me
With a professionally wrapped
Little box.
Arrogant
Because terrified
Little schmuck
That I was,
All puffed up
With this celebration of *me*-
I actually said
"Anything in such a little box
Can't be too good"
Or words to that effect.
Upon opening
It disclosed
A very expensive

Enameled Schaefer fountain pen
And pencil
Fine pieces
Too good for a kid
And yet the classic
Bar Mitzvah present par excellence.
Boy Scout that I was
(As well, thank God)
I right away apologized
And said
"Well I'm wrong.
That's the best thing I got,
I guess that
Great things can come
In small packages."
Bob approved
My instant moral development
And the process thereof really –
Disclosing my susceptibility to learning,
And smiled.

Lesson learned.

"Chipping"

In later life
A diabetic
He could not drink
The 30 year old
And even 50 year old Scotch
That only he could get
And would take
The tiniest, tongue-tip wetting
Dip

To remind himself
Of the past glory
Of this stuff.

I thought this silly at the time –
After all, if you can't have
This stuff
Why tantalize yourself
To agony like that?

But diabetic too now,
I do this myself -
Gustatory *memento mori*
Of former days.
    -   It matters.

Cigars

A connoisseur of the fine cigar,
– In the 50's he gave my father
Exquisite pre-embargo Havanas
Por Laranagas
Which I would steal
At 17,
Acquiring the taste.
Another gift.
For the rest of my life

He never gave up the Havanas
Now illicitly bought, vastly expensive.
He was all about taste,
Precious taste:
Redeemer of pain,
Reaffirmer of life.

When I'd visit him
In Brooklyn
Infrequently over the
Long years,
Living as I do in California now,
We'd quietly smoke together,
Rhapsodizing in silence
In the slate blue smoke
Of the fine Cuban euphoria:
A communion of sorts.

One of these visits
Was stupidly dramatic.
Out of the blue
I called without warning
From the subway
Near his apartment
And though caught short,
He gallantly recovered,
Though surprised
And invited me over
Anyway
Because I lived so far away
Because it was me.
We smoked.

The Apartment, In Old Age

He lived to be 93 years old,
Widowed,
Alone but for his part time attendant
Sitting in that apartment in that
Old Brooklyn neighborhood,
Watching *Mannix*, his favorite TV show,

Smoking his Havana,
Now a long time contraband,
Sometimes wearing his Cavanaugh straw hat
Regarded as the single best, most elegant make
From the stylish NY company
Even then generations defunct
And fearing nothing,
Because of his
God of Israel.

Bar Visits

On occasion,
If he felt up to it
He'd walk on his cane
To the neighborhood bar
For maybe the smallest amount of one beer:
An old, old man, wishing civilized
Manly conversation in public.

Death

When,
Taken unwillingly
Out of his beloved apt of 65 years,
To live upstate
With a son concerned for his care,
He died in 3 days.

The Bohemian

Bob was thus the bohemian of his generation,
Or outlaw of the family in his day.
When it was even harder,
A poet who liked my poetry

Though his own was gracefully entrapped in sentimental,
Rhymed 19th Century lyric.
A dealer in *"objets"*
Who kept his transactions secret,
Always suspected by the family
Of prevaricating and declaring
Bogus objects valuable.
He too was marginalized and made suspect
By the "burghers"
Of the family.

Le Envoi

These two realities,
The thirst for beauty,
And that he too was somehow
Ostracized,
Was "outlaw" –
Became planks
In the fragile platform
Of my hesitantly burgeoning self.

That,
That
Is light under the door –
Big time.

ROY

Decades later
I visit my cousin Roy
Abe's and Lilly's one child
The one they were told they could not have
And of whom
When born –
Abe said:
"Ahh, I'd eat his shit
On rye toast!"
When told
That babies needing "changing"
Could be, well, "aromatic"

This favored only child
Grew up to be a naval Captain
And submarine commander.
Cut from the same cloth as his father, -
My odd Jewish relatives,
With the blue suits and guns.

At my visit to my now retired cousin
After a separation of 37 years,
(We actually computed it)
I tell him
That neither he nor his family
Ever knew the insane and horribly
Painful severity
Of my life growing up.
And he says:
"We knew. We knew"

Contentious,
I want to challenge him
As starkly unbelieving as I was
 - How could they know? –
The veil of family secrecy so complete –
But somehow I stay quiet:
His eyes tell me
He knew,
They knew.

Now he tells me
That he'd always felt the family
Never understood *him*
Nor his choice of vocation.

Stunned, flabbergasted,
My jaw literally agape
I expostulate too loudly:
"What the fuck are you talking about!!??
They talk about you like you were a demigod –
'My nephew the sub-captain,
With the nuclear torpedoes
And the *"schvartzas"* to serve the coffee!'
Jesus Christ Roy,
To them it's like
A distinguished
Doctoral degree, only with macho!"

He says:
"Yeah, yeah, I know all that.
 But they never understood me
They never understood what I do!"
Or why I do it,
If I had followed my second choice of career

- Which was journalism -
They might'a understood."

He too felt lonely and abandoned in this way
And this was simply
The most strengthening
And emboldening
Thing anyone
Has ever said to me
Bar none, because
He, at the top
Of the family totem pole
Of esteem:
Awe inspiring – worshiped,
And I, vocation poet
Solidly at the bottom - reviled
Are both misunderstood
By the *rest of them*
And feel identically
Lonely and abandoned
In this way.
This was
And continues to be
A sacred moment
In my life:
The gift of a lifetime.

At this visit
A billion years
After my childhood
And youth,
My Cousin Roy
The sailor
Gives to me

His late father Abe's treasured
Copy of a 1913 edition –
Of Kipling's, "Departmental Ditties"
The proverbial "slim volume of verse"
With Kipling's personal seal embossed in gold
On crumbling red Moroccan:
The grazing elephant's head
With the swastika inscribed just outside and above
His circling trunk.

Along -
With the endless
Entangling fascination with words
-Let it be fairly be admitted-
From my father the lawyer -
What is my legacy
From my cousin the sailor
And my uncle the cop?

A book of poems,
And the mantle of poet.

Light, pure light
Though
The crack in the door:
A long time coming.

Envoi

These are dead.
Dead.
The light remains.

FURTHER TALES

MY BLUE HARLEY

I'm happy with my blue Harley -
          George Gershwin (paraphrase)

Backward turn backward // O time in thy flight// Make me a boy again// Just for tonight"
          Elizabeth Chase Akers Allen *

Time was, I had to have a motorcycle. *Had* to have one. 1959: in a small town in Pennsylvania, where I was working at as a counselor at a nearby children's camp, there was a Harley-Davidson dealership. Going there religiously on my days off, I fixed upon one motorcycle - a floor model, a demonstrator, with a paltry few miles on the "clock" and hence less costly than it otherwise would have been. It was smaller than what you'd conceive a Harley to be, only one small air cooled cylinder. A 2-stroke, where you put the oil right in with the gas, lubricating while being consumed. And no suspension in the back. A "hard tail". Primitive. All this on a far smaller frame than the big bikes, a miniature, but it *was* a motorcycle and it *was* a Harley. It was blue, Skyline Blue. I'd borrowed 5 Cs from Paul, a college pal which I never paid back. He died in the interim of leukemia at 37. So Paulie, this is for you. ..

My first solo ride was in those SE Pennsylvania hills, on the dealer's license plates. with a death grip on the handlebars and my whole body commensurately clenched like a fist. I had not yet learned to ride, to relax and ride. To ride.

I couldn't ride it to NY, didn't know how, no license or insurance. The dealer trucked it to NY for me, in the back of his pick-up truck. As I neared the apartment building, I got in the bed of the truck and mounted the motorcycle. A sort of pugnacious and triumphant arrival. I thought I looked like a float in the Macy's Thanksgiving Day Parade for small motorcycles. Kids in the street were agog.

I couldn't park it on the street, no license again. But where to put it? Why in my bedroom of course, in the 3rd floor bedroom of the apartment. The motorcycle was light enough to take on the elevator.. Of course *they* were scandalized, but you can't *"throw out"* a $500.00 object. One time the doctor came to see my ailing brother, - we -were still in the era of housecalls,- and my father, embarrassed lest the doctor (that paragon of Jewish respectability) see the anathema of a motorcycle in my bedroom, physically manhandled it out of the room into his bedroom to conceal it. . He didn't know how to handle it, and "threw out" his chronically painful back. My brother and I were laughing our asses off, and my brother claimed it cured him. People would ask: "Why do you have a motorcycle in your bedroom?!" And I'd answer "yeah, I drive down the hall and take a right at the kitchen for dinner." My sour acidulous cousin Irving, a bitter frustrated prick because he was forced to take over the family manufacturing business when his father was imprisoned for fraud during the War, thereby preventing him becoming the chemist he wanted to be - still asks on such utterly rare occasions as I talk to him "Are you the one with the motorcycle in your bedroom?" - this being outrageously immoral. Thwarted jealous bastard. On a beautiful fall day, the riotously varicolored leaves blowing in the cool and autumn wind, the sun shining gloriously I rode ecstatic on the NY Throughway to Vassar College in Poughkeepsie, NY, for a collegiate weekend date with the roommate of a girl I knew from Brooklyn. I wore long hair, black jeans, a red flannel shirt, a WWII style brown American bomber jacket**, white silk flying scarf, cordovan desert boots, light blue tinted bubble-goggles, a goatee and a white crash helmet. An apparition.

I had forgotten or didn't know that proper young gentlemen were expected to wear tie and jacket at meals in the elite Ivy League and Seven Sisters Colleges, of which Vassar was one. So there I was at dinner, red shirt, no tie or jacket, long hair, beard - wholly unacceptable. No one of the girls nor anyone in authority would actually *say* anything, so there we were at a side table, ostracized before the fact. My date was a scion of a proper New England family, but a bit of a rebel and we enjoyed ourselves immensely amid the hostile and condescending looks ricocheting off the walls.

The practice there was that the girls rode bicycles from place to place on campus. Overtaking a bicycle in front of one would occasion the girl wanting to pass declaiming - likely is a patrician New England accent - Paaaaasing Left, or Paaaaasing Right. And as they allowed cars on the campus along with the bikes, I reasoned they would let my motorcycle on too. No such luck: not allowed. I had wanted to overtake the girls on their bikes and say Paaaaasing Left, and Paaassing Right and pass after gunning the engine loud - VROOM VROOM!

The young women were allowed to "put up" their dates on these collegiate weekends in a dorm/hotel especially dedicated to the visiting young men: read Yale law students. I was accorded the "minimum" accommodation, a sort of attic garret room. Perfect. Time came to leave, and the valet would deposit one's luggage outside of one's room. . My luggage such as it was, was a pair of attached toy saddle-bags for a boy's bicycle. In cheap, thin black and silver plastic, of western saddle bag design, squarish, a little oblate, straps, buckles, lid folding over top, with the traditional decorative frogs. - bought for me by my late cousin Alfred for $3.00 in Colonia, NJ when I visited him on my way to Vassar.

Tableau: at my door I find a large, exquisite hand-tooled Moroccan leather valise with the tag "Steve Goldman" attached. Investigating, I happen to look down the hall to its other end, to see another guy, faultless in his Harris Tweed jacket and rep-stripe tie. He is dangling from a pinching thumb and forefinger my saddle bags held well away from his body, as though they contained bubonic plague. Sure enough, we had the same not uncommon Jewish name, Steve Goldman, and the valet had made the understandable mistake. The urge laugh, to succumb to nigh incontinent hysteric laughter was nearly overwhelming, but I managed to contain it for the poor Yalie bastard's sake, beyond a weirdly stretching smile. Maybe he took it as a grimace. No words were exchanged as we exchanged uh, luggage.

The motorcycle, a Harley, a true Harley, not an imported small displacement Italian bike *(Aermacci)* with Harley badges, H-D's marketing strategy to counter the excellent smaller displacement Japanese bikes -"rice burners" - then flooding the market. My love was primitive and small by Harley standards, meaning relative to the big displacement "Hawgs' so iconic then and now on the American road. As noted, my rudimentary lawn- mower 2 stroke engine required that the requisite dose of oil be dumped right into a newly full tank of 1 and ¾ gallons. The gas tank cap cover had a little steel cup welded right to it for the purpose. As the tiny one-dose cans of oil from Harley were exorbitantly priced, I took to carrying two WWII Army canteens strapped to the bike, one for water to drink and the other for a quart of the light two-cycle oil, available cheaply from gas stations by the quart.

One night I had to fill the tank, and there was one tank's dose and a little more in the oil canteen. So I filled the cup and poured it in, leaving a negligible amount in the canteen. Not enough to save and I certainly couldn't *drink it*. So I poured in into the tank. Why? Because of my insane food-training as a child. *Clean Plate Club.* Had to eat any leftovers not deemed worth saving. "Please darling, don't waste food, the children in Europe are starving! Eat, eat Darling. Eat for me." Food was not so much considered substance to feed human beings as humans were being deployed as machines to consume food. And it carried over. I put too much oil in the tank, and the machine never ran right after that. The too-rich mixture fouled the one spark plug, which remained fouled until it dawned on me (duuuh!) to change it. This brings us to the next episode.

There was only one place in Brooklyn and maybe even in NYC c.1961 to get a spark plug for the exotic 2-stroke Harley, Sam Cardinale's Harley Dealership in Coney Island. I knew I'd meet some tough customers there. This was not a matter of "colors" flying outlaw clubs a la Hell's Angels. Those guys were founded right after the War, but being a California phenomenon, we didn't have them "back-east." These guys were individual and say, collegial outlaws, pretty much by definition merely in virtue of riding, except say, if you were a cop. You didn't *"Meet the nicest people on Hondas"*** yet and J. Edgar Hoover had only recently and sneeringly called organized outlaw bikers the 1%! I feared that the guys, doubtless hanging out there and working on their machines would eat me for breakfast. Me, the college boy with the miniature Hawg with a windshield (!) and a crash helmet no less: Yech - unheard of!

So pulling into the yard, yes, there they all were. Big guys, classic big 74" inch engine displacement machines of the day. Not exactly Ivy Leaguers. One big quite clean-cut guy, a NYFD fireman with a 74 bored out to 90". (O the passion!)And a couple fairly hoody guys with immaculate machines, and one grubby, Italian guy. This guy, in an athletic undershirt, hairy shoulders, grease stained pants. (O, the penalties of love), cheap cigar clenched in his jaws and astride a flat black greasy Hog, dismounts and comes over to me. "Jesus Christ" I thought: here it comes! He asks me "Ay, izzat a Harley?" "Yeah" I say" And he says: "Sheesh! I ain't never *seed* one dat small! Have a beer!" extending a chilled, newly opened bottle of Budweiser.   So help me God.

Once, riding to Manhattan from Brooklyn for a date with a beautiful but ultimately silly girl I knew from school, I was on the very steeply rising and O so curving on-ramp to the Belt Parkway with the traffic crawling bumper to bumper toward the Big Apple's delights of a Saturday evening. I shifted down to get better purchase on the hill and avoid stalling, and in the bikes' slight speed retardation, the guy in back of me hits my rear fender. No harder than an emphatic pat on the back, or one of those light congratulatory punches you give a guy on the arm.

And that was all it took. Bike goes over like a pancake, thrusting me toward the top of the retaining fence 300 feet above the Gowanus Canal. Instinctively I crouch up into a fetal ball, hoping this would somehow lower my center of gravity and stop me from going over. I don't know if this worked -   I didn't know the physics of a body's gyrations in mid air,**** but I didn't go over. I bounced from the fence to the ground on my side, uninjured but in shock. I stand up, and automaton-like I turn down the throttle, which is at full rev in second gear and under no load (the unengaged rear wheel spinning at a million miles per hour) as the screaming engine (God knows how many dangerously excessive rpm) is about to reduce itself to steel powder. This Harley had no automatic return spring in the throttle. I tear off the mostly severed part of the windshield and toss it over into the Gowanus Canal.

I am about to pick up the bike when the guy *in back of* the guy who hit me, *the second guy back that is,* appears and very pugnaciously announces: "*Ay c'mon Mac, you're holdin' up traffic!* I go instantly nuts, and began slowly advancing on him- dressed as the as Vassar Apparition from the episode above." What? What did you say"? - with my worst Richard Widmark killer menacing look. This time in shock, I mean it. . And the guy does the greatest double-take I ever saw. Suddenly docile - "Uh I'm sorry man uh - say you need a witness?" Me: *No go away. Just go away.* The guy dissolves. The guy who hit me is standing by, white faced. Him I tell him: "fagedaboudit". I got back on the motorcycle and went where I was going, the girl's apartment in Greenwich Village. Four hours later, the PTSD hit me and I began to shake like a shutter on an old abandoned barn in a gale, even with a glass of whiskey in my hand.

I lost her in a snow storm. On my way to a party in Brooklyn later, she cut out and I was able to walk to my destination. In the interim, it snowed. When I walked back, she was gone from where I had parked her. Speculation was that the Dept. of Sanitation hit her with a snowplow, and that these guys bury their mistakes. Ah my love, how merrily I rode along.

Long gone: At 75, I covet replacing that bike. Yeah, yeah, I know its crazy.

Long gone. But just today, 3/17/14, - St. Pat's 54 years later in California, - I see a brand new big shining regular Harley parked, (and they now have an immense 103 cu. in engine) - and it had the real, adult version of my toy saddle bags - western style, thick black leather, slightly ovoid, commodious, gleaming chrome studs and trim - and the frogs. It took me back; O did it take ever me back. How merrily I rode along.

* *The original reads "*...a child again..."*
.
** *The jacket was made of course by the same Cousin Irving at his Long Island factory. I was forbidden the absolutely requisite black leather motorcycle jacket with all those rakishly slanting zippers, as this bespoke to "them" the "hoodlum" Italian kids, and the Nazi's penchant for black leather. In my freshman years at college, I remember going to the bathroom at a screening of Marlon Brando's The Wild One, and seeing guys 7 deep at the 5 urinals wearing them. Room full of guys in black; leather motorcycle jackets: no exceptions but me. 40 years later or so, I got one by myself. Debt of honor.*

****Honda's image scrubbing ad slogan of the era.*

**** *Much later, c.2014, I learned from a trapeze guy I ran into that you can indeed control the motion of your body in mid-air.*

The Ride

They were all almost hysterically anxious about me driving with any of them in the car. This was according the Angel of Death, the Uncontrollable One far, far too much power over them. As such, this probably never otherwise took place. The single instance I can remember is my father's trip home from a hospital.

He had had a cerebral or stroke related event, such that he was compelled to hiccup ceaselessly. This might be funny for the first 30 seconds or so; then you realize it can kill you. He was hospitalized and the incessant hiccups continued. The eminent English neurologist attending him allowed as to how medicine had known about this for 75 years but was at a loss to explain its mechanism. It had been noticed however that if, during a siege of hiccups the patient were to sneeze; this ended them for a time.

I occurred to me that if sneezing was induced it might be helpful. How do you induce sneezing? Why snuff of course - the old custom of forcefully inhaling powered tobacco through the nose and into the sinuses. So I ground up some of my mother's desiccated Herbert Tarryton cigarettes. Oddly, she, who was so afraid of everything, readily complied, perhaps realizing that even a negative result would be harmless. We administered this to my father. Nothing. No result.

I conjectured that perhaps real snuff might succeed. This was in the turbulent '60's and the Brooklyn Jewish Hospital (where I was born incidentally) was a middle-class island in a surrounding ghetto. There was police tape all around the hospital. As I strode out of the hospital, candystripers looked at me with a mixture of awe and fear; and old Jewish lady volunteers grasped my clothing and importuned me:" Please mistuh dunt go, it's too dangerous.!" Horseshit.

On the same block, not 30 yards away, I found a little Puerto Rican bodega and tried to order snuff in Spanish. How the hell do you say "snuff" in Spanish? So I invented an expression, ordering *"polvo de tobacco"* "powdered tobacco" if you will. "O, si, si!" And he produces two little aluminum canisters, identical, it seemed to me to those for 35mm camera film. Snuff: one of them mentholated no less.

George sniffs a pinch in each nostril, sneezes. Instant cessation of hiccups! It *was* the much finer, talcum powder like consistency of the snuff, after all! Never thought it was an immediate permanent cure, but not long afterwards, he was stabilized enough to be released. He had been the hospital 60 days and lost as many pounds. I probably saved his life. Never a word of thanks.

So this is about the trip home for him upon release from the hospital, and the unique oddity of the whole family being together in the car with me driving. I do not know how this was allowed to take place.

They were both seated in the back seat. My mother, who never really drove, and whose level of anxiety made her effectively afraid of everything, which I made up to call "omniphobia" kept shrilling: "Look out for that car. Look out for that car!" She literally did not know what she was talking about.

My father, emaciated, bundled up in his overcoat, pajamas and an astrakhan hat, would croak in his hiccup strained voice, "Toin here! Slow down! Toin here!" Because he could not relinquish control.

My brother, in the front passenger seat was leaning tensely, apprehensively forward, a sort of reverse cringe, not physically like Dad's repeated mock cringes, enacted in broad mugging burlesque when I walked by him, "serving notice" that I was a blustering, heedless dangerous person who would imminently run into something or someone, breaking it, him or her.. But my brother was in real terror, nearly off the seat.

When I could stand no more of this, I glanced over my shoulder to look at them safely for a second, turned back to the road, and in my best, strong, warm paternal Midwest airline pilot baritone announcing voice said:

"Good afternoon, lady and gentlemen. This is Capt. Goldman coming to you from the control deck of a privately owned Oldsmobile Super 88. We are flying at exactly sea level on this beautiful morning. On your left, off the port wing, don't fail to notice the plant-kingdom glories of the Brooklyn Botanical Gardens, and to your right, starboard, across the street, Brooklyn's Fabled Prospect Park."

"I'm sure we'll continue to have a pleasant flight, given a little less bullshit from the passenger manifest."

No one laughed of course.

The Near-Fight on the Dock

I worked intermittently as a longshoreman for 7 or 8 years on the docks of NY. I worked in truck bodies and freight cars, never stepping foot into an airplane or a ship. In the 40' trailer of an over-the-road semi rig, a tractor/trailer, the protocol, loading or unloading is 2 guys per truck, one in the rig, stacking or unstacking the "*fuckinfreight*" (one word and always referred to as such –), and the other on the tail, taking in whatever is delivered to said trailer, or delivering the now unloaded freight to the cart receiving it for distribution to its end users.

One night (always somehow night or graveyard shifts for me, less "choice" perhaps to senior and union guys – though I preferred them) – I'm working in a truck body with an Irish guy, a career longshoreman. You get to know one another at least casually in this kind of situation. So the guy asks me what I did before this, and I told him I'd been in graduate school in Canada doing an M.A. in philosophy but that I'd needed a break and so now I was here.

Like a pool of gasoline erupting from a lit match thrown into it, this guy flies instantly into a full red rage. Shouting:

"Why you sonuvabitch – I bust my hump 20 years on this fuckin' dock so I can send my kid to college to get what you got and you piss it away!"

He is running over fast with balled fists and the rage flashing from his eyes. This one is already "on". I step back and put up my hands. I don't want to hurt this guy, and I don't want to be hurt, and will take such measures as I can to ensure both, but who knows? I may have to behave more extremely than I'd like. Maybe this will be the world's last relatively harmless gentlemanly fist fight. But who knows?

When:

When an older longshoreman, in fact the oldest guy in the *"jernt"* - most of the time a fork-lift operator, a semi-honorific accorded to career guys getting too old to "hump freight." – we called him "Father John" – appears and intercedes – actually now standing between us. "Now wait a minute Bill, he's got his own way 'o doin' things and this is his call." Bill's rage dissipates as quickly as it had slammed on. "Ah, I'm sorry Steve, I was outta' line" and offers his hand. Of course I readily shake it.

Just another incident between two gallant American laboring men.

WORK ACTION

During the mid 60's, I worked for three consecutive Christmas Seasons in the great department stores of New York. During the accelerating holiday shopping and ensuing crowds, they put on temporary extra help, including junior executives, of whom I was one.

One Christmas at the iconic Macy's, I worked in its legendary Toy Department. Until the advent of FAO Schwartz, the Texas giant, it was the greatest toy distributing facility in the world. It was there that the first department store Santa - "the miracle on 34th St." - appeared. I myself had been taken there, sat on his knee, and told him what I wanted for Christmas.

There were 13 of us, each assigned – in restocking mainly – to one of the toy sub -departments – that is: genres of toys. On a night shift in the Christmas snow, cold and darkness of street we were of course unattached eccentric young men with college degrees. We generated titular nicknames, based on our "toy specialties". I was both the Doll King and the Plush Toy Prince; another guy was the Bulk Toy Baron and so on.

We would screw around constantly as men, especially young men, do in such situations. In the midst of Christmas, the cold and loneliness, we were surrounded by goofy child vectored displays, some animated. Kafkaesque vaudeville. The nicknames, the banter, the incessant wising - off - remember this was New York, - a brief vogue in ambushing one another with Air Blasters - a crate of which from last year's season were discovered. A large pistol like affair. When discharged it would issue a loud report and a palpable and forceful blast of air. You'd walk around a fixture and be ambushed by a colleague, and vice versa. College graduates, major dept. store execs.

One time I found a doll, again from the year before, that rarity, it was a male doll. Called "That Kid", articulable, about 10" high, he was accoutered as your typical country kid. Faultless in his tiny accurate jeans, the red and white checked shirt, the blue baseball cap, the tiny impeccable sneakers, and freckled face. And a scale plastic wishbone bean-shooter in his right back pocket, just begging for tinkering with. So you turned its arm, and THE GODDAMNED THING TALKED!" "Hey! That's ma pitchin' arm!" You out the bean shooter and: "Hey, put that back, ya big ape!"

So we executed it. I found a faux halberd, a long poleax weapon decoration from last year's Mediterranean Festival promotion, and we beheaded it with suitable "grave" ceremony. Head on the block and all. College boy shenanigans.

And we "execs" had at our disposal 7 grey jacketed stock "boys" - all black, all ex- Marines, all just back from Vietnam. Silent, distant menace. Perfectly compliant with work orders, they almost never spoke. Once, I heard one guy quietly discussing with a colleague his technique for killing somebody with a thrown knife. Some of the most dangerous men I'd ever been around. Looking back at so long a remove, it comes to me only now what assholes they must have thought we were, with our Air Blasters and mock beheading.

On occasion the following scenario took place. At 3:00 AM sharp, all the elevators doors opened simultaneously, (a statistical impossibility during normal daylight "sales" hours, this) each disgorging 2 or 3 guys. - cops, a stark surprise show of force, drawn pistols and brandished high powered rifles, open radios and Macy's famous security Dobermans straining at the leashes. The dog handler cops had Doberman head patches on their uniforms. I guess this was a kind of *prophylaxis* by fear, against theft. As the Xmas Day neared, I'd see $500,000 in raw cash on the carts to deliver it "upstairs", once the hidden safes - concealed and integrated into the childish displays - some moving -, maybe a Mickey Mouse fixture, or a squirrel biting into a walnut - were emptied, every accumulated $500.00

We had been told in our training that if anybody represented himself as a security cop, to ask to see his badge. Responding to this uniformed apparition of terror, - (of course they all screamed "FREEZE!" in chorus the second the elevator doors opened) - I absurdly asked the first guy "Let's see the tin!" (Cop slang for badge). The guy glared, grimaced and nearly snarled, but he showed me "the tin".

We 13 kid executives were overseen by one guy -an angry, stern, unsmiling, moonlighting regular Airport cop. I think that if the Toy Dept. did well that year, he was in for a whopping bonus, and maybe a job on Macy's highly coveted Security Force. We called him "Iron Jim" and Jim was out to run a tight ship to say the least.

One night early in the morning, as soon as I exited the elevator, he comes over and menacingly says "Goldman, see me in my office after the shift!" I think this was because I was 10 minutes late, or maybe some earlier peccadillo.

So I tiredly respond: "Aw Jim, if you're gonna fire me, why not do it now and save us both the trouble?" "ALL- RIGHT, GODDAMN IT, YOU'RE FIRED! GET OUT!" Me: "Fine!" He saunters off! As I spin on my heel and approach the elevator from which I just came, 3 or 4 of my colleagues who'd been eavesdropping nearby come over and: "Doll King - what's goin' on?" "Ah, Jim fired me!" "Yeah, the hell with that, we'll see about that!" they say nearly in unison! One of them, a Puerto Rican named Jose, an airman in 'Nam and a wildman with a flair for vaudeville shouts: "OVER HERE BOYS, ON ME, ON ME!" Or some other rallying cry. From all over the huge floor they *all* arrive by us in an instant! "What's goin' on?" "The Iron Man fired Steve." "Yeah, well bullshit!" And to a man, they declare a strike, a work action. Even stodgy Leo, The Negro Who Couldn't Jump, who wanted to be an accountant, in his perpetual 3 piece suit - - signed on without hesitation.

"C'mon you guys, don't worry about it! Cool it and save your jobs." say I. They're having none of it, the strike is in place and Jim is promptly informed. His threats availed nothing. This had to be "taken upstairs", and I mean *"way"* upstairs. You just don't shut down Macy's Toy Dept. as Christmas nears.

I remember the rattled national corporate vice-president in his robe and silk pajamas alighting on the floor from one of those same elevators, having been driven in in his limo from his mansion in Queens and accompanied by some of those very same cops, also in consternation. With a deadly serious look on his face he asked what was "up" and the boys, not me, told him. He then repaired to Big Jim who was standing apart and conferred briefly. Glowering, veins visibly pulsing in his forehead, Iron Jim had to relent. A spontaneous and paralyzing work action, without my intent or permission but wholly successful, had taken place on my behalf in one of NY's most high profile business locations. This would have been on the front-page of the NY Times otherwise. Jim was a far more tractable boss from then on. It was the 60's, and we were no one to fuck with.

A Tale of Two Guns
For Brendan Constantine

There is a story which ensues from this tale. In Macy's in '66 I was again a temporary Christmas executive charged this time with re-stocking the rapidly dwindling seasonal inventories in 7 departments. One of these was the Sporting Goods Dept, which in '66 - just before the racial conflagrations in the cities, carried guns. Not pistols, which in NYC required a complex procedure for obtaining a special permit which only a judge could issue. (This of course subsequently became meaningless.) No, Macy's sold "sporting arms" long guns: that is rifles and shotguns.

One day some unusual merchandise came in. In individual cardboard boxes, gaily and colorfully decorated with almost comic-book western scenes, cowboys, horses, high desert landscape. You'd think these were Daisy B-B guns for boys. Not so. Winchester 100th Anniversary commemorative edition rifles of the (original) Winchester Model of 1866, or Winchester '66 - the first dependable repeating rifle, the storied gun that "won the West" - and the one in all the cowboy movies.

And wasn't it lovely. Accurate in every detail, except chambered for the current cal. 30.30 cartridge, it had a blued steel octagonal barrel. A presentation piece, it had gold plating on both sides of the receiver assembly, suitable for engraving. And it was only $125.00, which amount I had in my pocket and had my hand around. I was *this* close to buying this beautiful piece of Americana. But then I guess my mother, miniaturized and dwelling in one of my ears said - or at least I heard: "What does a 27 year old Jewish poet with a pot belly and shambling around NY need a cowboy gun for?" So I didn't buy it.

Flash forward about 25 years if you will, say to in the mid 80's. Some construction guy I worked with in California had an AK-47 for sale. A Chinese copy, it too was a lovely piece, with very close machined tolerances, and a hardwood stock with beautiful lacquered straight grain and a gracefully incised aperture therein, ovoid and smoothly finished to form a built-in pistol grip. And this one was only $75.00 which I also had at the time. Again I was tempted but the voice I heard, this time my own, said: What did I need with a copy of the world's premier retail mass murder weapon?

I think in both cases, the temptation of the forbidden was at play.

But the point here is that I have always regretted not buying the Winchester, and not buying the Kalashnikov I don't regret at all.

Picture
For my mother Pearl Goldman

I always said that
I never saw my mother
laugh or smile in the
66 years that I knew her.

but I remembered today
that there was a photograph
of her at 23 holding me -
a six week old neonate
taken by her brother, an
amateur photographer - an
8 x 10 flat black and white close up in soft
focus against a background of a newly
greening Prospect Park in
Brooklyn in the light
spring of '39, and she is
sweetly beaming

The War was to start in 4 months.

THE WAR

WWII ALBUM:
Snapshots, Still Frames: All I Got

To those who fought it; To those who endured it. To those who died, were wounded or sustained loss. And to everybody else, that it should never happen again.

INTRO: MYTHOS. PREFACES

"My mother, the war."
Thomas Pynchon
(A character in Gravity's Rainbow)

"..swathed at birth in the wrath of the womb's blood..."
Steve Goldman
(From the poem The Hammer in the Sky)

I was born on the 8th of May in '39 the
year the War was to begin
and the day it was to end in Mother Europe
6 years later to the day,
To be called V-E Day evermore.

Born thus
my mother was The War
And raised so,
My first 6 years owned by the war,
I became The War and
My name is World War Two

I was born and raised by The War.
I fought WWII every day
Virtually from my birth
Until 6 years of age exactly

and every day thereafter until
August 14, 1945 V-J Day -
When the Japs surrendered
To end The War.
And every day thereafter that.
And as I write this.

I was born and Hitler marched: September 1, 1939. I grew fond of humorously announcing "I was born and Hitler marched" - as in "I was the cause of the War", a "commentary" on my horrible family's notion of me, and in general as it were, what I was brought up to believe.

Again, I was born and Hitler marched
On the brave Poles on *Sept. 1, 1939*.

(Put this poem aside now
And read W.H. Auden's
Great poem of that very name.) [1]

Whether or not you do
The ancient Greek philosopher Heraclitus
held that "war is the mother of all things".
We, the "Class o' '39 -   we and we alone are
Exactly his children and so marked:
The Children of Heraclitus.

To recap the Mantra:
I was born and Hitler marched,
20 months later, when I was 2 years and 10 months old
The Japs bombed Pearl Harbor.
I am the War minus 4 months.
I am the Armistice, the Peace in Europe
Minus 6 years to the day

I am the War at all
Minus 6 years and 4 months.

More numerology: born before the zero in the year 1940,
The last digit of my age is one more than that of the given year.
Thus, I was born in Year -1 before the War

For me, for the War
And perhaps for the World,
'39 is the Year Zero:
May the years
Progressively increase for the better.

Repetitive isn't it?
It is for me too.
The War is endless.
Let it end here.

HEADLINES

For more than 6 years and then some, the newspaper headlines were about nothing else. The world was about nothing else: and I was about nothing else. War in the entire world, read universe. And always the war in the family.

- **HITLER ANNEXES SUDENTLAND!**
- **HITLER MARCHES ON POLAND! WAR!**
    Brits Evacuate Children!
- **ENGLAND DECLARES WAR ON AXIS!**
- **FLYING TIGERS OPERATE IN CHINA!**
- **COCKLESHELL COMMANDOS SINK**
    TONNAGE IN DIEPPE HARBOR!
- **BRITS RESCUE 40,000 AT DUNKIRK!**
- **LEND-LEASE!**
- **U.S. SHIPPING SUNK BY SUB WOLF PACKS OFF EAST COAST!**
- **FRANCE/PARIS OCCUPIED!**
- **BRITS BATTLE IN SKYS OVER ENGLAND!**
- **JAPS BOMB PEARL HARBOR!**
- **WAR! "DAY OF INFAMY!" WAR ON JAPAN DECLARED!**
- **GERMAN/ITALIAN AXIS DECLARES WAR ON US!**
- **CORIGADOR FALLS!**
- **BATAAN DEATH MARCH!**
- **FREIGHTERS BRAVE MURMANSK RUN!**
- **MARINES TAKE GUADALCANAL!**
    Losses Grievous!
- **DOLITTLE RAID BOMBS TOKYO!**
- **AIR FORCE FLYS THE HUMP IN CBI!**
- **ROMMEL PLUNGES DEEP INTO AFRICA!**
    N. AFRICAN CAMPAIGN PROCEEDS
    Siege Of Tobruk!
- **EL ALEMAIN: YANKS AND MONTY VANQUISH DESERT FOX IN N. AFRICA!**
- **AFRIKA CORPS RETREATING!**

- **SOUTHERN INVASION: ITALY- THE BOOT!**
    Sicily, Salerno, Anzio, Montecassino,
- **ROME FALLS!**
- **GERMAN SABOTEURS CAUGHT!**
- **OFF LONG ISLAND/FLORIDA!**
- **FLEET TROUNCES JAPS AT MIDWAY!**
    Course of War Seen Turning!
- **BARBAROSSA: HITLER BREAKS PACT: INVADES RUSSIA!**
- **SEBASTOPOL BESIEGED!**
- **KURSK: GREATEST TANK BATTLE! NAZIS SMASHED!**
- **STALINGRAD HOLDS, NAZI WINTER WAR IN RUSSIA FLOUNDERS!**
- **MACARTHUR KEEPS WORD:**
    Returns To Philippines!
- **GREAT MARIANAS TURKEY SHOOT!**
- **US FLYERS KNOCK OUT RABAUL!**
    Brits, Aussies, Poles Hold Out!
- **ALEUTIANS WATCHFUL:**
    Invasion From Japan Feared!
- **NAZI COMMANDOS RESCUE MUSSOLINI!**
- **BIG 3 ALLIED POWERS MEET!**
    Teheran, Dumbarton Oaks, Yalta
- **NAZI ROCKET WEAPONS STRIKE LONDON!**
- **MASS BUILD-UP IN ENGLAND!**
- **8TH AIR FORCE POUNDS SCHWINFURT, PLOESTI,**
- **VIENNA, BERLIN: Casualties At 300%!**
- **D-DAY! INVASION! ALLIES STORM NORMANDY BEACHHEAD: LODGEMENT MADE!**
    (6/6/14 D-Day + 70 years as I write this.)
- **ALLIES MOVE INLAND: HEDGE FIGHTING COSTLY!**
- **OPERATION MARKET GARDEN FAILS!**
    Arnhem: A Bridge Too Far!

- PARIS LIBERATED!
    G.I.s greeted by Wildly Joyous French Crowds!
- MILLIONS OF DPs ROAM EUROPE!
- BREAKOUT AT BASTOGNE:
    Bulge Finally Won! Terrible Toll!
- YANKS ADVANCE ON GERMANY!
- RAMAGEN BRIDGE INTACT!
    Army Enters Germany!
- YANKS MOP UP AROUND MAINZ!
- ARMY TAKES TRIER!
- MARINES TAKE IWO JIMA!
    Fighting Fierce! *Flag raising on Mt. Suribachi*
- DRESDEN FIREBOMBED BY US, BRITS!
    Carnage Recalls '37 Rape of Nanking!
- ARMY UNITS LIBERATE DACHAU, BUCHENWALD!
    Elements of Our Nisei Troops Among First To Arrive!
    (The Headline That Never Appeared.)
- THE CAMPS: UNIMAGINABLE HORROR: STARVED BODIES AND THE DYING IN THE TENS OF THOUSANDS!
    Ike Wretches!
- YANK AND RUSSIANS IN HISTORIC LINK UP AT TORGAU ON THE ELBE: GERMANY FINISHED!
- HITLER DEAD!
- GERMANY SURRENDERS! V-E DAY! *(My Birthday!)*
- ATOMIC BOMBS! HIROSHIMA, NAGASAKI LEVELED!
- V-J DAY: JAPS SURRENDER! WAR OVER! PEACE!
    The photograph of the sailor kissing the nurse in Times Square.
- BERLIN AIRLIFT! PLANES LAND EVERY 9 MINUTES TO FEED STARVING GERMANS!
- UNITED NATIONS FOUNDED!

How I Became the War: Lore - Personal or My Complete Environment: "The Home Front"

Here's how. Then, the City of New York's Rent Control Commission allowed apartment dwellers renewing leases a paint job or new wall paper per room every three years. Thus during my first conscious three years at all, my bedroom, later to be shared with my brother, displayed boy's room "Army" wallpaper: light brown background, approximating the military khaki, decorated repetitively as wall papers are, by crude drawings of Army combat scenes, a soldier running, his bayoneted rifle held aslant in front of him, some guys serving a large artillery piece, and a tank cresting a desert dune or berm. The second year, we had the cognate "Navy" wall paper, light blue background, a battleship firing its immense primary guns, planes taking off from a carrier, and a sub in the deep. I was surrounded by the War. Don't get me wrong, I wanted this: boys are romantics. (Read on to the parts about "Cousin" Buddy below.)

With 17 million under arms, it seemed every 7th guy and woman or so in public was in uniform. My father give "lifts" to any uniformed hitchhiker in the street and on the road. He never did before the War and he never did afterwards. The effect of this on me speaks for itself.

Our rear kitchen window gave on the courtyard, a paved empty space in back of the building which bordered another such courtyard, that of the next building, such that their 3rd story rear kitchen window opened upon ours through the clear and mild summer air. . They had an adolescent daughter, Rene, who played the piano and sang. With both windows open, I would see and hear, Rene playing and singing loud and clear "Praise The Lord and Pass The Ammunition" and "Comin' In on A Wing and Prayer" - popular war songs of the time - over and over again and nothing else. Perhaps these were the only songs she knew. Sitting at my kitchen window watching and listening to Rene, I loved every minute of it, every time.

For the 1939 World's Fair in NYC, a copy of the Magna Carta was brought over by the English to represent them in their exhibit, The War was imminent or had actually started, and it was deemed safer to leave it "over here". It was stored at Fort Knox, next a copy of the Constitution until 1947. As the radio commentator 85 years later said: "They had a lot to say to each other".

It is said that the first American casualty of the war was an elderly Jewish man who was an Air Raid Warden who fell off a 6 storey building in the Bronx while making his rounds in an air raid drill. With American involvement immanent or already begun, he wanted "to do his bit".

We did not know until '43, my mother told me, that we had a chance of winning at all. Imagine the anxiety they all breathed minute to minute and what was relayed to the children, however tacitly.

And I remember that around then, say when I was 4 or 5, going shopping with my mother in the A & P Market, and that she had books of ration stamps, and those dime-sized red and blue "OPA" tokens. She told me she had to have these to buy certain things; mere money was not enough. I was aware of scarcity and rationing: meat, sugar, coffee, cigarettes, and gasoline. The sense of threat of privation came through to me from my mother.

And the Camps, I cannot speak here of The Camps. You already know. And we did not know about The Camps - the Holocaust, until '43 either, my mother said as well. . O she also said there was news beforehand but nobody believed it. Ike puked at the gates of the first of the Camps he saw. This raised the already vastly high anxiety in a Jewish household.

Across the street was a nursing home (as they were then called) which my father represented. It was owned and run by a woman, who had a younger brother, said to be a quiet bookish boy. Drafted, he became a marine. This kid had been in the island fighting and survived. When he came home, he embraced his sister, and broke 2 of her ribs.

Somehow we were in Times Square one time and there was a white plaster Statue of Liberty 10' or so tall. I asked my father "what is that?" "Statue of Liberty" and amid the streaming crowd, I thought it was really Miss Liberty: The New Colossus Herself. I was awed: the grandeur and the sheer size of her. I was about 4.

On April 12, 1945, some neighbors on the floor, English people incredibly, rang the doorbell. Mother and child, little Estelle my age, 5. With tears and the classic British quivering lower lip and choked up the woman stammered "Th Th The president's dead!" My mother was shocked and hurt and burst into crying. I was very frightened.

As children we played "Guns" in the street, really playing WWII. "DA DAA - got ya, ya dirty Jap! Take that ya dirty Kraut!, RAT-TAT-TAT-TAT! Got ya!" "Did not!" (Somebody had to play the enemy.) "Did too!" etc. On the rare occasion one admitted to being "hit" - this for the sake of authenticity - an elaborate and acrobatic "death" would ensue, gasping grotesquely, clutching the abdomen and with all kinds of gyrations, falling "dead". In one variant, you could be "killed", lie on the ground, count to 50, and arise a new man. This mostly when we needed kids to play.

During one such session, Richard Rosenbaum's gun, (we were about 4) broke. It was a sort of nondescript toy lever-action cowboy gun which made a sound, much inferior I thought to my own faithful, miniature balsa wood Springfield rifle, with a working bolt to actuate the "Click" upon "firing". My father, standing around and ever handy, fixed it. Shortly, Richard's father, Merc came by to thank my old man. That is how they met. A rotating weekly Wednesday night Pinochle game ensued, for at least 25 years to the mid 1960's or so. My old man, living to 90, was long the last survivor. Of this game, one member, a German Jewish merchant who kept scrupulous records announced that after 25 years, playing "nickel-dime" cards, about 15 cents had changed hands. (At 4, Richard Rosenbaum, later a lawyer, was my first friend. He is gone now.)

I remember my father's oldest brother, Uncle Herman, who didn't drive, trudging over on foot in at night in Brooklyn. He died far too young from a heart attack, alone in the street in the snow. He died at age 44, or was it in 1944? My father's second oldest brother, the cop written of heretofore, was a police captain and the Harbor Master of New York. What must have that entailed during the War?

My father had civilian defense jobs. He worked at the Brooklyn Navy Yard in the ship-fitter's shop. Although a young lawyer he actually worked on refitting the battleship USS Missouri and wrote his name on an inside face of an armor plate. When the foreman found out he was a lawyer, he was given some kind of little electric scooter to carry messages around the Yard instead.

Before or after that, he became an Air Raid Warden, His job was to go around the block seeing to it no lights were left on during the "blackout" - during air-raid drills, dangerously and illegally, thus providing target for any German bomber. He was issued a WWI helmet, the shallow "tin pot" painted white with the triangular Civil Defense logo (CD) painted on the front, an armband and a short billy-club. Right after the War, my mother threw out my wartime treasures from my father. Their presence must have been painful to her.

My friend John's late mother was a "Rosie the Riveter" during the war, working on planes. Except that her name wasn't Rosie, it was Eileen. And she wasn't a riveter. She operated a drill press.

Early in the War, the NY skyline gave illuminated contrastive background to the periscopes of the German subs viewing surface merchant ships. The "wolf packs" were already sinking American shipping from stations 60 miles off the shore NY.

Italian POWs were held at a fort facility In Brooklyn. They were friendly and glad to be out of the War. The local Italian/Americans brought them cakes, handed through the perimeter bars.

My mother's best friend's brother, a captain, was killed in his tank. My mother visibly shared Marcie's grief. She wept with her friend Marcie.

My cousin Leonard Weinstein, then an ensign in Naval Intelligence at the combined Coast Guard and Navy facility at Amaganset, Long Island was close to the investigation that led to the capture of the German saboteurs in 1942, who were landed clandestinely there by submarine and rubber boat. His desk was next to that of an Assistant District Attorney in civilian life from Brooklyn, who broke the case using laundry marks from shirts worn by the English-fluent saboteurs who had lived in the US before the War. Of the 8 German saboteurs apprehended, 6 were sent to the electric chair. Of course we knew nothing of this then.

We had a "shirttail' relative, "Cousin Buddy" - son of my father's best friend Moisch the Dentist. He was a fighter pilot, of a legendary P-51 Mustang, the beautiful and a most advanced such plane we had, and ever after a personal icon for me. A nice Jewish boy, he would dutifully come visit his "aunt and uncle" on furloughs during the war. He'd appear in uniform, Army Air Force, with his 50 mission "crush cap", his pilot's wings and captain's bars agleam: my supreme hero. Little boys idolize soldiers during their country's war and especially airmen, who do greater damage to the enemy at profoundly greater risk. "Off we go into the wild blue yonder..."

But Buddy never went to war; even though at 4 I thought he'd personally shot Hitler. He was an instructor pilot (IP) in Florida, teaching other guys how to fly '51s. Only the best guys become instructors. The reasoning is that if they teach others to be more effective, they save lives of our boys while making them more deadly against the enemy. (It is something the military does well, be it pistols, bayonets or hand to hand.) A handsome boy of average height,(you can't get giants into WWII *fighters,) he was courtly and respectful to my parents. I worshiped him and can weep today thinking of him. After the war, he gave me official AAF Pilot's Recognition Manuals, one for planes and one for ships. Oak tag loose -leaf books, bound with a brown army shoelace, to be balanced on a pilot's knee while in flight to tell them as best it could with pictures, schematic drawings and silhouettes what to shoot and bomb, and what not to. These books were still classified - a fat fuck these heros cared about that kind of thing after the war. I'm talking supreme boyhood treasures. When I asked him worshipfully what the most dangerous thing he'd done was, he answered "Towing targets". That is where the instructor plane tows a target 400 yards behind him which is fired at by the trainees following, using live ammunition in aerial gunnery practice. It <u>is</u> quite dangerous.*

Why the Mustang? As a child in the mythic dream time of the war, no greater evil than they, no greater good than we, I loved our righteous cause and planes and aviators especially, because these cowboy soldiers of the skies could wreck such tremendous damage on the enemy from the air, at the greatest of risks to themselves, and of these none greater than fighter pilots, who flew alone", "God is my co-pilot" etc. The mystique of the aviator. (The 8th Air Force's bombers in Europe sustained greater casualty rates than the rightly storied Marines in the Pacific. Some squadrons had 300% per cent casualty rates.) ("We live in fame or go down in flame, Shout: Nothing can stop the Army Air Corps!") The Mustang was introduced late in the War, our best fighter. And my cousin flew one. To this day, the P-51 remains a personal talisman.

Similarly as with the recognition manuals:, after the war, the guy who married my physical therapist from when I had polio in '49, took my brother and me, kids, on a day's outing. He had been a tail-gunner in heavy bombers. He let us drive his new car - my brother on his lap steering and me, sitting on his right working the pedals. We rode jauntily around NY's Chinatown. It was the real thing. Sid supervised us only the bare minimum. The thrill of this illicit and illegal escapade was exhilarating beyond telling, consummately so given the twin household regimes of the suffocating safety fetish and terrifying legalist fundamentalism where we lived. It is exhilarating to this day when I think of it.

In '45, when I was barely 6, I was nestling with my father on my bed, listening to my radio. It was a little white Arvin AM radio he'd bought me. It cost 6 dollars. The radio made the first disclosure of the atomic bomb to us, broadcasting it. It must have been news about the Hiroshima bomb although I can't say for sure. My father, always the brave tough guy, with ever the near pugnacious attitude, hung his head and softly muttered. " OOO". He may have actually said "Everything will be different now." Anyway I knew this, but not how, except that it meant everything and that it was very bad.

How I Became the War: Lore, *Or:*
A Vet Told Me:
"Over There"

(Again, there were 17 million in uniform then. They are dying now at the rate of a thousand per day)

I some time ago developed a personal ritual. If I spotted a Vet (biggest tip-off a baseball cap saying WWII Vet, on a grey head), I would approach and say:" Thank you for saving my Jewish ass" and ask him (in one case her, a lady marine) where they served, and what they did. Answers are cordial if not detailed. A typical first response is "We had a job to do." On parting, after have been given the anecdotal information, and already having shaken hands, I render a slow, grave and perfect salute.

But one guy answered "I saved my own Jewish ass too." One of so many gray haired octogenarian vets, he was a Polish Jew, who had been a Spitfire pilot in the RAF's expatriate Polish Squadron in the Battle of Britain, - the Blitz- and he told a wonderful tale. One day, on a non-combat mission, he had to fly from London to Scotland. A woman in uniform asked to come along. They had sex in the single-seat fighter plane, she sitting on his lap.

The British had a Jewish Brigade, Jews from Palestine etc. They fought in Italy. In one instance, a soldier, a Corporal Schwartz I heard, stormed a German bunker shouting: "Raus Deutshce Schweinhunds, der Juden sind heir!" (Get out you German "pig-dogs" - the Jews are here!)

When I worked for the Civil Service in the '60's in NY, I was in the break-room with an older Jewish man from Europe who had been interned in Dachau in '39, before the War. He said he hadn't been treated badly. Flabbergasted, I expostulated "Dachau!!?? Well, how was the food!?" At which precise moment, Lenny, a new-hire kid who was ambitious and trying to make a name for himself - entered the room to hear only that incredulous remark. He promptly began excoriating and upbraiding me for such callous disrespectful abuse of Mr. Schwartzenbaum. The old man and I both rolled our eyes, and of course, we all, all 3 of us, were Jewish.

The brother of the single lady across the hall came back from Europe. He had been a combat medic with Terry Allen's "Timberwolves". He became a doctor after the War on the GI Bill. 14 years later, I was taken to see him during one of my earliest and most terrifying bouts of depression. Like the rest of us, he couldn't know what was happening to me, nor fix it.

A few years after the War, we were in the car with a young vet friend who my father was sponsoring to be a lawyer. He had been n the Pacific, and could not be swerved from the opinion that the Japs were fanatical lower animals, because "you would wake up in the morning and find your friend with his throat cut, right next to you." He told me "might makes right" - the first time I ever heard that. My most passionate 9 year old liberalism, humanitarianism, and staunch democratic ethic - i.e. .rather that "right makes might"- all from how I had been brought up - couldn't swerve him from that either. But I think my old man was distantly proud of my precocious skill in argumentation.

A marine vet told me that when he was stationed in China after the War. (I didn't know of marines in China) They were guarding Communist Chinese prisoners, but didn't have enough men, so they used Japanese prisoners of war (the surrendered enemy) to guard the Chinese, (the ally) with their own captured weapons, provisionally re-issued to them by the marines. The Japs, as honorable prisoners of war cooperated.

I met an English guy who was Royal Marine at Tobruk, where he survived without getting hit. A movie guy, he was later in the movie by that name, the one with James Mason as Rommel. He was an extra playing a German soldier, of all things. Some other extra stupidly let the muzzle of his rifle down in the sand, where it picked up a pebble. This guy emerged from Tobruk without a scratch, but was seriously wounded in the movie Tobruk when the other extra fired his "blank" cartridge at him and he was hit by the pebble, now a ballistic projectile. The doctors said he escaped paralysis by a half inch.

One Army unit in Italy drilled in walking side by side few feet apart. and holding their weapons at waist height to discharge them rapidly while advancing evenly in line, which was supposed to" mow down" enemy soldiers hidden in the woods. This tactic was never used.

An airman I knew saw an Me 262, the German Messerschmitt 262 Sturmvogle or Storm Bird, the first operational jet fighter, which could travel at an impossible 550 mph. He did not tell his colonel for fear he would be considered crazy and hospitalized. The same guy told me about a P-47 Thunderbolt fighter somehow recovering from an excessive power dive with burns on the cowling from the immense air friction. Speed estimated in excess of 700 mph, this was perhaps albeit unintentionally the first supersonic flight.

Gen. George S. Patton ordered one of his officers Maj. (later General) Matt Abrams, with a tank and crew to depart from the main line of advance of the 8th Armored Division, to rescue the general's, son-in-law from a prison camp, which I believe he did. I met a vet whose infantry unit marched within 40 miles of a German concentration camp where his brother was interned, and he knew it. A private, there was nothing he could do. Our main American battle tank is named after Abrams as of this writing.

(3 Sayings)

General George S. Patton swore aloud that when he got to the Rhine, he would piss in it. When he did, he did. The picture of it exists.

When the 101st Airborne Division was dangerously encircled in Bastogne during the "Battle of the Bulge", its commander General Anthony McAuliffe was offered a "dignified" surrender by the Germans. He is reputed to have said "Nuts!" to the German officer making that offer under a white flag of truce. What he actually said was "Shit".

<u>*Montgomery to Churchill*</u>*: "I don't drink or smoke, I get 8 hours of sleep per night and therefore I am in 100% form.* <u>*Churchill to Montgomery:*</u> *"I drink a quart of brandy a day, smoke cigars around the clock, I get 4 hours of sleep at night, and therefore I am in 200% form!" But what he really said to Montgomery was ...drink, smoke, sleep etc. "And you're working for me."*

* * * * *

I heard of how the tail section of a B-17 Flying Fortress heavy bomber was severed near intact from flak (antiaircraft fire) and how the now entrapped tail gunner, unable to parachute, "flew" the section, which with its tail planes intact resembled a rudimentary unpowered airplane to earth, by shifting his weight around, and survived.

In Brooklyn in the 60's I met and befriended a Russian Jewish barber, who had been in the War in the Russian Army. A lyrical soul, he had been in many horrendous battles. He once told me: "At Smolensk, you coodvalk across de river on de bodies". He once related that he'd parachuted 3 times into battle. "O" I naively said "Aron, were you a paratrooper.?" He said "I'm not a "<u>jumpeh</u>" but tree times dey kick me out of plane on mein Kopf." The Russians didn't train these men for parachuting; they simply gave them parachutes and ordered them to *jump into war. They accepted a 15% casualty rate just on landing alone, broken legs etc.*

A friend told of an uncle in the Navy, who was cutting a bulkhead when a big wave hit the ship, causing him to lose control of the torch which described a perfect circle cut on the metal, whereupon an officer appeared and commended him for his good work.

It is more widely known that a Pharmacist's Mate operated on an acute appendicitis patient in a submerged submarine in the South China Sea, which was under depth charge attack by a Japanese surface vessel in 1942. There was no doctor on board. With officers holding the patient down, with kitchen knives for scalpels and a bent spoon as a retractor, whiskey being the only anesthetic, the guy operated. The patient survived but was later killed in action shortly afterwards. The "surgeon" survived the war and lived into his 80's.

It is told that shortly after the War, two young men, who had been junior Army officers in the War, encountered one another in a bar. They had not met before. Telling "war stories" at the bar, the former infantry officer told of how he and the unit he commanded were trapped in a cul de sac in a German town, with a German tank already advancing up the street toward them. He allowed as to how "we were already dead" when miraculously, an American fighter plane appeared in the lower sky and "took out" the tank. (The P-51 Mustang fighter plane carried 5" bazooka rockets, an anti-tank weapon.) In the course of conversation, they were able to ascertain with certainty the date, the town, the street corner and the time of day of the incident. The other guy was the pilot.

I knew an old guy who had a little job carrying beer in cases from the delivery truck inside to a local bar in Venice, CA. The job was a sort of sinecure from his from his friend the wealthy bar owner. Unattached and otherwise impoverished, Roger lived alone in a small room. He had been an Army captain in the war, in command of black troops and he was looked down upon and castigated by his fellow officers for leading mere "niggers". Roger said long after the war: "Once you get to know them, they're just like anyone else."

When the Americans liberated Paris (Aug. 19, 1944), the great soprano of her era Lily Pons stood atop an American tank and unaccompanied sang Le Marseilles. Seemed as though there was not a dry eye in the non-fascist world.

A doctor who had served in the Pacific told me of how sulfa drugs, the only anti-biotic they had was not metabolized and how it could be distilled and used again from the urine of patients initially treated with it.

The heat of a battle of close engagement found 2 Army surgeons, one German and one American, in the same bombed-out house, each working impartially and feverishly on the wounded of both sides, without regard to the nationality of each patient.

In his book "Wartime", the critic, academic and writer Paul Fussell who was a young Army officer in combat, reported seeing a German house with the front wall entirely blown off with almost surgical precision by an artillery shell, with the whole family, killed instantly by the shock wave alone but not otherwise wounded, unmarked and plainly visible close to the postures of their family roles: Dad in an easy chair, Mom in the kitchen, the children at play undisturbed, as if frozen intact in that family tableau of death.

Somewhere on the inner wall of a church in France, something like this was seen scrawled: "July 17, 1917 and December 4, 1944. I hope never to see this place again. Eugene V. Smith, Chicago, Illinois."

I just learned this past week, in July of 2014, 69 years after the fact, that my cousin Roy E. Goldman (1925-1997), later Capt. USN. (retired) - the submarine commander, written of earlier in this book, served in the Army in WWII, as a M/Sgt tail gunner in B-17 Flying Fortress heavy bombers, flying missions over Germany. This is the most stunning disclosure of my life. Roy: thanks for saving my Jewish ass and your own and those of the whole family.

AFTER THE WAR

Nakano

A friend of mine, a Japanese-American woman, told me of her late father's service in the War. He fought in the legendary 442nd Regimental Combat team, the single most decorated unit in the history of American arms, composed entirely of Japanese men, Nisei, *while their families were imprisoned in concentration camps here at home. My friend told me of a story-sized memoir he'd written, telling of a love affair.*

In telling me about the piece, my friend mentioned that while fighting in France, these troops were given short "R and R" interludes in some kind of subterranean shelter, which had running water, a library, a movie theater and other domestic amenities. This was puzzling in the extreme. When I read the poetic, the lyrically beautiful piece, this facility turned out to be a little used section of the Maginot Line itself, though the Line was still occupied by the Germans overall! These Nisei *had to station guys outside, to engage Germans who could come by with flamethrowers and satchel charges. They lost guys that way too.*

Then Pvt. Tom Nakano, on a furlough in Nice fell in love with a French woman who in turn loved him. They knew they would never see each other again. The woman was a prostitute, but thus, his respite from the War was love, not merely sex.

Another Soldier

This is the last entry to this book, included only weeks before its publication. I am home for 2 days as I write this in late August of 2016 - after 7 weeks in a rehabilitation facility, for therapy addressed to a disequilibrium and an attendant tendency to fall. I could not stand up for fear of falling. I was re-learning how to walk.

My bed was right next to that of a Japanese American man who looked to me to be of WWII age.

I made him out to be 85; he was 96. He was quite hard of hearing and lucid but spoke very little.

I asked his visiting wife, a charming woman of 87 if her husband had been in the Army. O yes she said, but that was during WW II. Not wishing to appear intrusive, I asked her if he's been in the legendary 442nd or the larger unit which contained it, the 100th Battalion. She did not know. I subsequently asked his son and a grandson. They were unsure as well.

I tried to elicit this information from the aged gentleman himself. Initially, I had been saluting him in his wheelchair as he rode by. He always saluted back. I began by asking him directly, mimed 442 with my fingers and eventually drew a large 442 on a piece of legal paper. When shown this, he wanted it so I gave it to him. I was still unsure. About 3 days later, I realized what I should have done. In my deepest voice, and very loud – having been told that hard of hearing people more readily hear low frequencies –

I intoned to very loudly: **GO FOR BROKE!** *- the legendary motto of the legendary 442nd. And his smiling face opened like a sunburst.*

I was (and am) delighted with this. Unable to contain myself, I told it a night later to a nurse from the Virgin Islands. She countered with the fact that a late granduncle of hers, one Luther Swayne has been a Tuskegee Airman, and how she herself had tended to him and his colleagues after the War: Mathew Shreezsus and Jerome Spurling.

Thus did the War follow me blessedly into rehab.

Jacques

I was in France once in '97, visiting an expat friend from Brooklyn. When first in Paris, he had to go and teach in the Sorbonne and I was left alone for an afternoon. I figured I'd go see the Louvre, and go I did. I didn't want to enter and see some of the great and voluminous art, pending a return someday, but rather tried to take in the vastly extensive grounds and numerous buildings – individually and collectively great works of art themselves, and even themselves far too much to appreciate in one day. I did what I could.

Having arrived there by bus, I'd been instructed to take the Paris subway, Le Metro, to rejoin my friend and host at his school. I did not know where the nearest station was. I began to ask passers- by, in my rudimentary French as needed.

The first, a well set-up woman in her 30's or 40's answered succinctly: I haven't the "foggiest." A British woman on vacation herself.

I accosted a bunch of Asian high school girls, thinking they were Vietnamese immigrant kids from the 13th Arrondissement - the chosen locale for these immigrants, where in fact I would later stay. To the question in both languages: "Tee heehee" – nervous girlish giggles. Japanese kids on a high school excursion.

I then approached a fellow I thought typically French. Standard tan raincoat, tie and shirt – no jacket but a V-neck sweater and one of those flat, brimmed, tweed workman's hats – think of the English cartoon character Andy Capp. Fellow about 70. In my very partial French, I inquired after the location of the nearest Metro station: "Pardon Monsieur, sivous plait, ou et le Metro?" Smiling he indicated he would walk me there.

He did, and led me across the Louvre's entire commodious front plaza, a distance of about 1/3 of a mile. I remember thinking I wouldn't have had a prayer of finding that station alone, and I had a deadline to re-join my friend. He walked me all the way there and even pointed which line I was to take of the 2, and I wouldn't have known that either.

Before embarking, I introduced myself: "Je m'appelle Steve" - and I asked him his name, "Monsieur, svp, comment vous appelle vous?" "Jacques" he said.

I thanked him politely, commenting on his generosity. "Merci bien Monsieur, vous et tres gallant. And asked him why he was so generous – why he walked me all the way when a simple verbal or gestural indication would have done. I have forgotten how I said this in French.

He answered: "Because the Americans were very kind to me during the War."

EPILOG TO THE WAR...INCIDENTAL

The War is the premise of the Star Wars series of films; and that premise is one of the entire universe was at war - civilization itself at stake, there being no choice at all but to fight to save and preserve it. This powerfully recalls the national mood and the effective national unanimity of feeling. Only one person in Congress (a woman from Montana) voted against our Declaration of War against them when the Japs bombed Pearl Harbor. And there were no doubts about our utter human goodness and the undiluted evil of the enemy. Nigh cosmic Good Guys vs. Bad Guys. Case Closed.

The cycle recapitulates the War in its major theme images for us, the enemy scowling in German grey (Feldgrau) uniforms, sallow, gaunt and ominous of visage - inhabitants of the "Death Star". And Darth Vader himself, uniquely black, weirdly voiced and faceless, the ultimate Evil Being: The Devil: Hitler.

But "Our Boys", for example in armed single seat spacecraft (read fighter planes - space fighter pilots: aviators again), "Off we go into the wild <u>black</u> - cold and empty yonder") - are handsome individuals, clean cut and even jaunty looking, in friendly brown uniforms: and defenders of "The Federation". One guy even looked Jewish and one guy was Black.

The decorative iconography and taxonomy are significantly accurate and evocative, right down to the level of visual detail and titular designation Note that the horde of faceless, identical, white plastic armored robotic soldiers of the enemy are "Storm Troopers". This is right from the Nazi lexicon:"the actual name for Hitler's shock troops from the "Brown Shirts" - the SA (Sturmabteilung). Note also that- their helmets in are the unmistakable and terrifying shape of the classic German- latterly Nazi "coal bucket" helmet, (Der Stahlhelm.)

ZAP! TAKE THAT! - YA DIRTY KRAUT!

But the war was not a mythic fairy-tale in the mind of a child, with gallant knights of the air or space gloriously vanquishing monsters. It was like all wars, a matter of dying invisible amidst rubble by the side of the road, unable to move or cry out, in what would have been screaming pain, with your guys right there, easily able to extricate and save you. But I have to believe it was, along with Spain, the one right War.

WW II Album: Appendix of Alternative Openings.

Below are 2 verses which may be substituted for the existing first verse. You may ignore this, substitute one or the other or both, or use either or both and the existing one. In short any choice, number, combination and order is up to you. Read your choice (or subsequent arrangements) aloud. Do not strive for elocution or theatrical phrasing for meaning. Mumble. Strive for a chant like or incantatory expression. Sing it tunelessly or read/recite in a soft monotone, slightly too fast. Try, *without trying*, to bring about a mild, continuous trance or reverie generated by your own non-ego mediated relation to this text, as you read, sing, intone or mumble it softly aloud, even softening the inherent stresses and rhythms. Then begin the rest of the poem in whatever fashion is normal to you, and indeed the rest of your life. Thank you.

    I
Born in Year '39
the year to beget the War
and the day the War –
Mother War
She was killed
in Mother Europe,
To be called V-E Day 6 years later
and evermore
as long as memory shall...

    II
Borned in '39 AD
The War was all encompassing to me
And borned on the 8th day of May
A Monday
I'd always thought it was a Wednesday
My birthday a witness in that way
To the forthcoming Victory-In-Europe Day

Or V-E Day as they would say
In Mother Europe now not so far away
That Day if I may
Then anyway
Exactly 6 years away to the Day.

GRAND EPILOG:

THEN

Kindergarten, 1944
After dancing around in a circle with the other children,
To the teacher's piano
And with the Victorian propriety taught us then –
I make my first leap of courage ever
And,
Never suspecting she will accede –
I ask Miss Duncan, that venerable Celtic dowager,
Ancient even then
"Miss Duncan, may I use the easel?"
This is the first assertive act of my life.

But "Yes, Stephen, you may."
Surprise now and fear.
How could she allow this privilege to someone so unworthy as myself?
And what will I do now? What will I paint; will it be good enough?

I paint a brown house
- Houses should be brown -
A crude square in swaths of brown tempera
With windows, a smoking chimney
A mother, a father, a yard, kids.

Who was I?
How did I render house and family?
I would trade the Mona Lisa
Could I but have that painting
Which cannot exist anymore
Except as molecules dispersed in the universe.

First grade: beginning reading
I don't get it,
How can those symbols be words?
Finally, it starts to cohere
With one small, seminal event:
The first word I ever actually read
Is "*is*"- an "*i*" and an "*s*" – "*is*",
From the verb "*to be*"
And the second "*it*"
An "*i*" and a "*t*" –
The thing itself.

I remember saying
All alone
To the cement wall
Beside the ramp
To the basement
Of the apartment building
Saying, pridefully and with feeling
In reverie –
Almost smug, self pleased
Almost as if rehearsing:
"I am 4 yeee-ars old!"

At 8 I have a fight
In the snow
Of the Blizzard of '47
With 8 year old
Herbie (later "The Oaf") Lieberman-
A huge kid who hulked and towered over me
And is now sitting on my face.

When my father strides over
To break it up –
A grim big man
Winter-bulked in
Dark wool overcoat,
Hat, earmuffs,
Those massive ladder-closure galoshes -
- Though scared and then vastly relieved
I say
Because I know he wants to hear it
"Dad I can fight my own fights!"
And he smiles.

I remember the searchlights
Like silent, stately scythes of light
Slicing and searching in the black skies
Of wartime NY
For the droning German bombers
Which thank God never came
- And the war forever incessant
In the family

I am in mourning forever
For the benign and lovely
Child I was.

MAIN ENDING

Notes to the poem "WWII Snapshots, Still Frames: All I Got"

1   Many notable poets, writers and celebrities too numerous to mention here served in the Armed Services during the War. But among them were: Tom McGrath in the Aleutians (For the American War Dead in Asia), Randall Jarrell (The Death of the Ball Turret Gunner), Louis Simpson (Memories of a Lost War), Richard Eberhart (The Fury of Aerial Bombardment), Lincoln Kirsten(Rhymes of a PFC) Simon Perchick (Bomber's Moon), Joseph Heller (Catch 22) in Europe; Ray Clark Dickson (Blood Chit) and James Dickey (The Firebombing) (in the Pacific) and Francis Dean Smith (work unknown) on the home- front. I urge you to read some of the greatly moving masterworks noted in parentheses above and many more by many more war poets and writers. Additionally, these will serve to enunciate the horror of war, and defray any childish fantasy of romance. And JD Salinger and Charles Schultz were on the beach on D-day, Yogi Berra, Tony Curtis and Lawrence Ferlinghetti offshore on naval vessels; Clark Gable and Jimmy Stewart and George (later Sen.) McGovern in the air over Europe, and on one such occasion, Walter Cronkite as a gunner. And Charles Lindberg flew missions against the Japs in the Pacific.

2   The "Headlines" are not accurately cited, and even so in only indicative chronological order, not perfectly so. Furthermore, some generically similar events are clumped together, which of course took place at different (sometimes widely separated) times, such as battles in a theater or locale, or say, conferences.

3   Because of who I am, because of where and especially when I was born, somewhere along the line I became an amateur anecdotal historian of WWII. Rigorous scholarly or academic military history, causes, campaigns, troop movements, strategy, grand historical interpretation are fine. But I wanted and want to know what happened to people, to see through their eyes, their experiences, their feelings, their memories when available.

A Laingian* Appendix, Optional
EXERCISES IN LANGUAGE PATHOLOGY

SUBTEXT / HYPERTEXT

One can almost say the Language
The "hypertext" really
Was "Ostensible English" -
Which used homonyms of English words
And parallel syntax:
Seamless evil duplicates
Of English words and structures
And grammar O so fastidiously correct.
But it was the immutable sub-text that counted:
Only one thing was ever said:
"You are an asshole
And you should die
For your presumption to live and
Ruin my life."
(My brother had permission to be born, I did not.)
"You are therefore, a piece of shit with moving parts."

A kind of family reductionism, -
But I repeat myself.

METALINGUISTICS

In this universe for example,
The expression: "that's your opinion" or "you're *entitled* to your opinion"
Means you are an asshole
Or a piece of shit.
Thus: -

THE LINGUISTIC ANALYSIS OF INSANITY

The Ontological Transmutation of Language or:
The Semantic of the Expression Transmuted Instantly
Through 7 Easy Stages

From English to "Family" or:
Black Magic from the Mouth

1)   When one of them stated for example that some statement by me was my *opinion, or only my opinion* or that *I was entitled to my opinion*: well then:

2)   If they had agreed with me, (rare, i.e. if I had the *"right"* opinion: i.e." *their*"opinion), the "matter" of *my opinion* or my *entitlement* thereto would never have come up.

3)   But should I maintain something they disagreed with, the focus was now "covertly" switched from the actual matter <u>at hand</u> (issue, topic, assertion, position etc.) to the "matter" of *"opinions,"* and the "matter" of *"entitlement."*

4)   Now, by sledge hammer innuendo, the word "opinion" equals "wrong opinion," and the statement "You are entitled to your opinion." means "You are entitled to your WRONG opinion."

5)   You have arrived at the wrong opinion (i.e. one different from *mine: the truth*) because you have (or are) a *faulty* or distorting perceptual apparatus, and, as sanity is a function of proper perception, you are thus crazy, or insane,

6)   That said, inasmuch as you are crazy and cannot therefore perceive correctly, hence your thoughts and feelings are inappropriate to anything real or important, and must be discounted utterly in serious human affairs. In other words, having produced them, you are damaged goods, a broken wind-up toy, malfunctioning of course.

6a)   Conundrum: You're nuts so you produce erroneous beliefs, and believing them makes you nuts. (A kind of family synergy.)

7)   Thus you are ontologically equivalent, for all intents and purposes, in terms of human value, to an object (not a subject), a thing, a piece of shit, albeit one with moving parts, or more politely: a wind-up toy. QED

THE DIALECTIC OF INSANE DEDUCTION.
The Linguistic Analysis of Insanity: The Processes

A REBUTTAL STRATEGY

Me: X, Y and Z are the case.

Them: That's only your opinion.

Me: How do you know?

Them: Well, you just said so.

Me: Yes, but I could be lying. Perhaps that's not my opinion at all. So you see, that's only your opinion that this is my opinion. QED

(Ed. note) Of course they could then allege that now, this was only my opinion that such was their opinion that said-same was my opinion, reciprocally ad infinitum, ad nauseam. Such was the nature of dialectical progress in the family. If on the other hand we were sane, it might have been more meaningful to say, "Well, this is my opinion of your opinion."

THE MATTER OF DOCUMENTATION, VERIFICATION AND SOURCES ETC. IN THE FAMILY

Me: X, Y and Z is the case.

Them: How do you know?

(Ed.note: Philosophically, the question "how do you know?" presupposes a range of possible answer-types, such as, for example:
"I saw it." "I read it in a reputable book." "Someone told me so, on good authority." "I had a strong intuition of it." "I deduced it." "Everybody knows it; it's common knowledge." "God revealed it to me in a vision." "It's a recent scientific discovery which I read about in today's newspaper and/or saw on television," - and/or anything else delimiting the unqualified range of answers the question would allow – whichever selection conventionally comprising one of the *kinds of answers* appropriate to *How do you know?)*

Me: So which of the aforementioned kinds of answer are you requesting?

Them: UTTER SILENCE. Just the original "how do you know?' tacit, not specified further. That, or the usual ducking of the question, by more obfuscation.

Thus, "How do you know?" actually means: "Since the assertion is false, *there is no way of knowing it,* and you merely *think* you know it, (i.e. it's your *mere opinion* that you know it) because of course, it being the case that you are a faulty knower, your cognitive apparatus is damaged, ergo you are insane, ergo you are a piece of shit, or at least it's equivalent in probative terms etc. etc. In all, this is an additional proof of the nature of your status, heretofore ascertained, QED.

EPIPHANY

The following is not hyperbole.
It was one day in the 60's
While walking down Harbord Street alone
On my way to a bakery
To get some real home style Jewish rye bread -
In Toronto where I was in graduate school
Taking high-powered philosophy courses in linguistic analysis
And philosophy of language
And pondering issues in these areas
That it *actually* occurred to me
That given its myriad of parts,
Arrangements, relationships, rules, structures
And inflections of various sorts
That language could also be used for communication.

End Appendix

*R.D. Liang, Scottish psychiatrist who wrote of dysfunctional relationships as "Knots" – in twisted aphoristic enigmas or puzzles.

OVER THE YEARS---STEVEN

Steven is a friend of mine

He reminds me of Frankenstein.

That was long ago

the monsters we two have fought

have faded like horse and carriage

Now Steven is more at ease with himself

and I also have changed

Unfortunately the trial was much more interesting

than the verdict. Dismayed "NA"

We are true friends, Always learning, always

gathering bits and parts of life together.

When we meet now, not as often as yesterday,

but when we do meet, we still compete

to fill each others cup with what we want

each other to keep of ourselves.

For when ever one of us goes for the long sleep

We will forever walk together

and

silently remember and keep.   LNB/H

(Leroy Norman Baker Hoffman)

Friends Forever
Leroy Hoffman Sr.
Christmas # 1987

AUTHOR BIOGRAPHY
Steve Goldman exists.

www.EdgarAllanPoet.com